FACE-IT
Finding Answers Concerning Every Issue Today

*Renewing the Black Church
by Reclaiming the Black Man*

DR. AVA S. HARVEY, SR.

WESTBOW
PRESS®
A DIVISION OF THOMAS NELSON
& ZONDERVAN

Copyright © 2019 Dr. Ava S. Harvey, Sr.

Interior Graphics/Art Credit: Dr. Ava S. Harvey, Sr.

All rights reserved. No part of this book may be used or reproduced by any means, graphic, electronic, or mechanical, including photocopying, recording, taping or by any information storage retrieval system without the written permission of the author except in the case of brief quotations embodied in critical articles and reviews.

Scripture taken from the King James Version of the Bible.

This book is a work of non-fiction. Unless otherwise noted, the author and the publisher make no explicit guarantees as to the accuracy of the information contained in this book and in some cases, names of people and places have been altered to protect their privacy.

WestBow Press books may be ordered through booksellers or by contacting:

WestBow Press
A Division of Thomas Nelson & Zondervan
1663 Liberty Drive
Bloomington, IN 47403
www.westbowpress.com
1 (866) 928-1240

Because of the dynamic nature of the Internet, any web addresses or links contained in this book may have changed since publication and may no longer be valid. The views expressed in this work are solely those of the author and do not necessarily reflect the views of the publisher, and the publisher hereby disclaims any responsibility for them.

Any people depicted in stock imagery provided by Getty Images are models, and such images are being used for illustrative purposes only.
Certain stock imagery © Getty Images.

ISBN: 978-1-9736-5735-4 (sc)
ISBN: 978-1-9736-5737-8 (hc)
ISBN: 978-1-9736-5736-1 (e)

Library of Congress Control Number: 2019903135

Print information available on the last page.

WestBow Press rev. date: 03/19/2019

CONTENTS

Dedication vii
Foreword ix
Preface xiii

Chapter 1   The Black Church and the Community 1
Chapter 2   The Black Condition in America 16
Chapter 3   The Injured Black Man 32
Chapter 4   The Healing of the Black Man 44
Chapter 5   Forming the F.A.C.E.-I.T. Fellowship 53
Chapter 6   The F.A.C.E.-I.T. Curriculum 64

Bibliography 87
About the Author 91

DEDICATION

To the omniscient God, my Lord Jesus, and the empowering ever-present Holy Spirit, my life belongs to you. Thank you for saving me.

To the most important man in my life, my father, Samuel David Harvey. I would not be the man that I am without you. Dad, you set the perfect example of manhood throughout my entire life. I watched you raise our family and provide for us with very little to spare. You worked hard both outside and inside the church. You kept a good name throughout the community. You prayed us through, kept us in church, taught us right from wrong and loved me and my mom and sisters with all that you had. No matter how high I get, I will always be looking up to you.

To my precious mother Bobbie, thank you for seeing the best in me when everyone else could only see the worst. You are truly a woman of prayer. I love you dearly.

To my beautiful wife, Leslee, I love you. I cannot explain how much your understanding has meant to me. You have provided me with the room and space to gather my thoughts and the time to put them on paper.

To my children Amari and Ava Jr., never give up on your dreams. Keep reaching, striving, believing and trusting in God. Always remember, your dad loves you.

In memory of our "Immortal Beloved" Evangelist Wanda H. Taylor, and Deacon Jessie Butler – forever in our hearts.

To my family, Mother Dorothy Butler, Latasha, Eric, Rosalyn, George, Tracy, Ricky, Donna, Craig, and all of my nephews, nieces, cousins, relatives, and friends, thank you!

Special appreciation goes to Dr. Megan Williams for editorial suggestions and directives. I am truly grateful for your insightful expertise.

To the FACE-IT Fellowship of Pastors and Men, you are the reason for this book. Together, we will change the world.

To the Pilgrim Rest Church Family, thank you for always supporting my ministry and providing the platform for me to work the vision that God has given me.

To every Black man in the world, I pray that this book serves you well.

FOREWORD

One of my greatest passions as an African American pastor and moral leader is ministering to the black male in the context of the black church. Many of the social ills that confront the black race have been squarely on the shoulders of the African American male. One of which is fatherlessness according to research done late last century. The absentee father is the culprit and basis of most social problems within our race such as suicide, behavioral disorders, rape, and substance abuse. Also, the high school-dropout rate, the incarceration rate, and runaways are all directly related to fatherlessness (Birks, January 24, 1996).

I found this data alarming in the late nineties while attending the Interdenominational Theological Center (ITC) and researching my dissertation project. Here of late, while reading David N. Moore's *Making America Great Again Fairy Tale? Horror Story? Dream Come True?: A Challenge to the Christian Community,* I discovered that fatherlessness is not only a cause but also a result of generations of segregation, ghettoization, job deprivation, housing discrimination, education discrimination, mass incarceration, over-policing and police brutality. In a word, African American males suffer from societal humiliation and shame (Moore, 33). Dr. Moore's analysis of their plight is in the same spirit and attitude that Dr. Ava S. Harvey grapples with in his book. He addresses the issues of the African American male and the greater need to restore the African American male's presence to the black church. Other research done in the late nineties also supported Dr. Harvey's analysis and resolution to the issues facing the black male, namely that:

> "Religious belief and practice contribute substantially to the formation of personal moral criteria and sound moral judgment" and that "regular religious practice generally inoculates individuals against a host of social problems, including suicide, drug abuse, out-of-wedlock births, crime, and divorce." (Fagan, "Why Religion Matters" 1996).

Dr. Harvey's book was very relevant to me as a pastor of two predominately black churches and as a chaplaincy director for the largest prison population in the state of Mississippi. Mississippi has one of the highest incarceration rates in the United States. Whether on the job or in the pulpit, I deal with men struggling with the very issues that Dr. Harvey has researched and sought to provide solutions for. His book, for me, serves as an update to the issues facing the African American male and the black church in this new century.

Dr. Harvey's approach is a historic analysis of the social, economic, political, and cultural issues of the black church and the black male and the challenges that each entity faces. He further provides solutions that are realistic and relevant for our times. Unlike so many, he didn't get caught up in what Dr. King described as the "paralysis of analysis," but provided a model and concepts to address the issue of restoring African American male relationships with each other, their families, their churches, their communities, and their Creator.

As a fellow pastor in Dr. Harvey's community, I find it very intriguing how he approaches the problems and his creative ways of finding solutions. It is a reflection of his shepherd's heart as an African American pastor and community leader. You can sense his identity with the African American male as a father, brother, son, and friend. This book is a great and informative resource for black clergy and all concerned about giving hope to black males and to the black race in general in an effort to find wholeness.

Dr. Jesse Kelly

Chaplaincy Director, *Mississippi Department of Corrections*
District Superintendent, *Jackson District Second Ecclesiastic Jurisdiction Church of God in Christ Southern Mississippi*

PREFACE

"Not everything that is faced can be changed, but nothing can be changed until it is faced."

– James Baldwin

Everyone throughout this life will eventually need the advice, counsel, and insight of others. Although God has given each person the ability to exercise the freedom of their will, our destiny is inseparably linked to other people. We simply cannot thrive when we isolate ourselves from others. The Black church has traditionally served as the unifying agent within the Black community. It was the locus of formation regarding morality training, spiritual awareness and activism. It provided a safe space for African Americans to heal from the wounds of slavery, bigotry, Jim Crow and both obvious and hidden discrimination and racism.

In recent years the role and place of the Black church in the life of African American people has begun to diminish. In no specific gender is this reality seen more clearly than in the absence of Black men from the pews. Across denominational lines, irrespective of geographical locations, backgrounds, and class, Black men are exiting the Black church at a rate that is shocking and alarming. The key to restoring the Black church lies in the hands of the Black man.

This book seeks to offer a new strategy to reach and resource the Black man. Chapter 1 explores the unique relationship between the Black Church and the Black Community. Chapter 2 examines and analyzes the overall Black Condition in America. Chapter 3 identifies the Black man's burden and his injury. Chapter 4 conveys a methodology of healing for the Black man. Chapter 5 introduces the F.A.C.E.-I.T. (Finding Answers Concerning Every Issue Today) Fellowship as a means of resourcing the Black man. Chapter 6 provides character lessons of the F.A.C.E.-I.T. Curriculum.

CHAPTER 1

The Black Church and the Community

A UNIQUE RELATIONSHIP

The African American church has traditionally served as the pinnacle of all things related to the Black Community. It has provided the platform for acceptance, identity, and solace from a world filled with bigotry and prejudice. It helped to unravel the ropes of injustice through the eras of Slavery, Reconstruction and Jim Crow. The Black church gave its people religious and academic education, while patiently teaching them how to read, write, and reason. Its place within the community allowed it to become a haven for social connection among its members and the primary jurist for acceptable and unacceptable behavior. To be a member of the Black church was to also be a good community member. Each family within the community was expected to join, attend, and participate in church-life until death. Today, African American churches are numerically and spiritually declining and it is imperative to adequately address the factors that are contributing to the regression.

The unique relationship that the African American church has historically shared with the African American Community is slowly unraveling. The relational ties began to evaporate as social, economic, and religious changes within society negatively impacted the Black family. There is a serious need to establish effective Spiritual Care to Black churches that are experiencing the residual affect of declining memberships, spiritual apathy and scarcity of new conversions. Consistent with Black church membership numbers declining is also the challenge of attracting viable spiritual leadership from the pulpit. African American churches often lack both the appeal and the funds to attract suitable ministers that are not self-serving at any level of experience. "Part of what we're seeing is a leadership mismatch of people who want to serve in larger churches in urban areas with larger salaries," states Reverend Marcia Clark Myers, Director of Vocation for the PC (USA).[1] The Black church once served as the main source of instruction and direction to the Black Community, but now, some believe it has become irrelevant. Peter Paris confirms:

> "Black Churches have had a prominent role in shaping, maintaining, and enhancing social order and communal solidarity by what sociologist call "adaptive" and "expressive" functions. In addition, they have inculcated in their people fundamental moral responses to such conditions which, while varying in accordance with the intensity of the adversity encountered from one time to another, nevertheless comprised, then and now, the authoritative basis for moral existence in the Black community."[2]

---

[1] Ned Barnett, Faith and Leadership – A learning resource for Christian Leaders and their Institutions from Leadership Education, Duke Divinity, (accessed August, 2016)

[2] Peter J. Paris, *The Social Teaching of the Black Churches* (USA: Fortress Press, 1985), xiv.

BEING REPLACED

"The African-American Church in America has stood between individuals and the larger society for Blacks for over two hundred years. In so doing it has been a source of empowerment and mutual assistance and a center for considerable social change."[3] The twenty-first century African American church seems to be "competing" with many other agencies and factors that have replaced its place of prominence. It is contending with media (television, Internet, cell phones, Facebook, etc.), careers (professional involvements, jobs, money), other interest (hobbies, habits, passions), relationships (marriages, dating, living single), idols (cars, houses, lifestyle), and time. As E. Franklin Frazier writes in his groundbreaking book, *The Negro Church in America*:

> "The Negro church can no longer serve as a refuge as it did in the past when the majority of Negroes lived in the South under a system of racial segregation in rural areas... Willy-nilly Negroes are drawn into the complex social organizations of the American community."[4]

Dr. Frazier also adds:

> "It was inevitable that the Negro should be drawn into the organized forms of social life in the urban environment. As a consequence, the Negro church has lost much of its influence as an agency of social control. The church has ceased to be the chief means of economic cooperation. The church is no longer the main arena for political activities which

---

[3] Thorn Moore, The African- American Church – A Source of Empowerment, Mutual Help, and Social Change. Published online 20 Oct 2008, 147-167 (Accessed January 2017)

[4] E. Franklin Frazier, *The Negro Church in America* (New York: Schocken Books, 1974), 76.

was the case when Negroes were disfranchised in the South. In a word, the Negroes have been forced into competition with whites in most areas of social life and their church can no longer serve as a refuge within the American community."[5]

Dr. Frazier directly makes the connection of urbanization (the dynamic migration of Black people from rural areas to cities, resulting in the dismantling of the Black community) to the overall economic shift of income within African American communities. Black people naturally transitioned from agricultural and farming sustenance to more lucrative, consistent, and stable income opportunities.

CHANGES AND CHALLENGES

"When we refer to the Black church or the African-American church, we refer to more than a particular ecclesiastical body, denomination or single organization."[6] There is little appreciable difference between many mainline denominational churches. Black Methodist may worship in different form from Black Baptist, but the similarities outweigh the negligible variations. "We have discovered no distinctive differences in the social thought of the respective Black Baptist and Methodist denominations."[7] From this understanding, all African American churches have something uniquely in common that unifies their struggle. The ties and binders of Black churches have historically been centered at the goal of preventing Blacks from having a distorted view of true Christianity and to serve as agents of personal, social, and economic elevation. The African American church in America was the gathering place for worship but it was also the place to practice collective thinking. As Dr. F. Keith Slaughter posits:

---

[5] Ibid., 76.
[6] Whelchel, Jr., *The History and Heritage of African American Churches,* xix.
[7] Paris, *The Social Teaching of the Black Churches,* x.

"The Black Church served as a haven for the enslaved and the formerly enslaved. There they found the psychological salve for their souls, safe space for the work of identity formation among each other, an anchor for their developing community and a voice to enunciate their longing for freedom and liberation."[8]

For over 30 years I have personally seen the detrimental decline and sometimes closure of Black churches that have slowly lost influence within their respective communities. From an up-close and tangible angle, to witness the devastating affect of the death of a church is extremely difficult to view, yet to not understand the reasons of its demise is even more unfortunate. The challenges appear to be the same for most, if not all, Black churches regardless of denominational affiliation and historical significance. Having traveled extensively as an annual itinerant evangelist (also known as a revivalist) to many Black churches and observing various church-settings in urban locations and rustic communities, I can clearly see that something is wrong. As an informed observer, I am seeking to offer African American churches a different set of options that may help to prevent the rigor mortis stage of physical and spiritual death from potentially occurring.

I have observed and noted several similarities within African American churches that are declining in membership and spiritual influence. One primary observation is the type of people who are consistently attending. These congregations are mainly composed of the Baby Boomer Generation (ages 50-69), the Silent Generation (ages 70-87), and very young children (below 18 years of age). Ironically, Generation X and the Millennials are the missing age

---

[8] F. Keith Slaughter, *Therapeutic Dimensions of Black Preaching* (USA: Get-Success Publishing, 2014), 97.

groups that are often glaringly absent in Black churches.[9] Besides the age group differentiation, through visual observance it is noticeable that very few Black Men are in the pews. These observations were noted as I attended various itinerant venues such as conferences and revivals.

Words have power and the manner in which they are used has influence. In order to have a clear understanding of key words, it is important to define terms in a manageable manner. While some may have difficulty understanding cultural terms and language deviation, my intentions are to provide an informational foundation for growth. Throughout this book, words that have more than one meaning are used. Therefore, I am defining the way in which I intend to use these keywords within the context of each section.

WHAT IS THE CHURCH?

Establishing a working definition for the term church is not as simple as most would think. The Greek word for church is Ekklesia, from which we derive the word ecclesiastical. Its literal meaning is an assembly belonging to the Lord.

> St. Matthew 16:18 And I say also unto thee, That thou art Peter, and upon this rock I will build my church; and the gates of hell shall not prevail against it.

Most religious scholars agree that there are two kinds of churches: Universal and Tangible. The Universal church is the spiritual body of baptized believers who have accepted Jesus Christ as their Lord and Savior. No one can "join" the universal church; a person has

---

[9] Pew Research Center : The Generations Defined. The Millennials (Born: 1981-1997), Generation X (Born: 1965-1980) Baby Boomer Generation (Born: 1946-1964), Silent Generation (Born: 1928-1945), Greatest Generation (Born: Before 1928) http://assets.pewresearch.org/wp-content/uploads/sites/12/2015/01/FT_generations-defined.png (accessed April 2017)

to be "born" in to it to become a member.[10] The tangible church is a congregation of people who meet in a physical location and are connected together for a multiplicity of reasons. The tangible church is the same thing as a "local" church.

There are literally hundreds of thousands of tangible (local) churches across the world. These churches are divided by location, regions, denominations, interest, doctrine, traditions, concepts, egos/personalities, agendas, goals, and in some cases race. Usually anyone can join a local church if they meet the criteria of the denomination or local assembly. For instance, within a Baptist church, a person can join three ways: Letter (a formal letter written from the previous church that the individual attended), Christian Experience (a person's testimony of having a salvific religious encounter with Christ), or Candidacy for Baptism (when a person seeks to be baptized in obedience to the Great Commission).

THE EARLY BLACK CHURCH

"The Black church is the oldest biblically-based Christian organization of African descent persons on United States soil; it owns its "Blackness" and its connection to the historical church as established by Jesus of Nazareth; it is the sustainer and nurturer of the faith and the training ground of African American survival."[11] The Black church in America has its beginning in the cruel sins of slavery, discrimination, and racism. However, long before the founding of the African Methodist Episcopal Church by Richard Allen and Absalom Jones in 1787, Black people worshipped outdoors, under brush harbors, and in the agricultural fields. African people knew about Jesus Christ before they were enslaved. In fact, many of the

---

[10] *To be born into the universal church is to accept the salvation offered by Christ's sacrificial death. Catholic and Protestant Religions differ in salvific beliefs regarding the "born again" experience but there is unanimity that the source of salvation is Jesus Christ.*

[11] Slaughter, *Therapeutic Dimensions of Black Preaching*, 179.

early Church Fathers such as St. Augustine, Tertullian, Origen and Athanasius were from North Africa and were people of color.

African people have always had a strong sense of spirituality that drew them to build temples, establish religious practices, and worship the Creator. However, the great sin of slavery and Colonialism reduced the humanity of Black people to the point of being soulless. Unlike the Indians who were proselytized by Spanish and French Missionaries, Black people were relegated to living as the beast of the field. If they were fortunate to attend a White church, they had to do so from the balcony or listen through open windows outside.

The Gospel was not preached to the slave as a means of redemption or regeneration, rather it was always a message of obedience to their masters. With the disadvantage of being illiterate, the limited vocabulary of words, and the absence of someone to teach them the truth of Holy Scripture, most Black churches in America were started under brush harbors. The basic tenants of their worship services were ring-shout dances, soul-filled hymns from the fields, prayer, and a brief message of hoping for a better day. What was happening within White Euro-centric churches was not happening within Black churches. While most White churches were studying the tenants of the Reformation and singing the words of liturgist in hymnals, Black people were seeking answers and hoping for justice. The Black church had a different mission than the White church and to misunderstand this truth is to make a very grave error.

THE ROLE OF THE LOCAL CHURCH

The role of the local church is to be the Godly agent on the earth that represents what Christ would do if he were here in the flesh. It is the place of evangelism, salvation, restoration and healing for the lost; and teaching, training and equipping for Christians. In any given service there is someone who needs evangelism, salvation, restoration, healing, teaching, training, or equipping. When the church biblically functions correctly; it is able to meet the needs of the people as the agent of Christ on the earth. Meeting the needs of others by definition is called Ministry. Yet the Black church's ministry expands beyond spiritual transformation, it also has to recreate the image of God within its people.

Most Black churches have never been able to get beyond the far-reaching grip of slavery and they spend the majority of time providing temporary comfort by offering hope of a better day. In some cases the perverted prosperity gospel is given as a primary means of receiving God's blessings. Consequently, a host of Black parishioners often do not have a solid biblical understanding of the primary role of the local church or a healthy Systematic Theology, Christology or Pneumatology.

THE BLACK CHURCH IN 15 YEARS

What will the Black church look like in the next fifteen years? Fifteen years from now, everyone over the age of 55 will be in there 70's and everyone that is 5 to 10 years old will be 20 to 25. Why is this important? According to the Centers for Disease Control, the average life expectancy for African American males is 68.6 and 75.5 years for African American females.[12] Therefore, the dynamics of the Black church will change dramatically in the next fifteen years. If the Black church does not have a Vision that makes significant progress related to the Black man, it will further lose its prominence.[13]

Any church that does not reproduce, gain, increase, or expand internally and externally will die. A local church with Vision must also find a balance in differences that exist between the realms of its members. Within every church there is a fight. People are fighting for what they believe and what they want. When I say that they are fighting, I do not mean literally; but rather they are fighting in their minds and hearts. Every church has 3 kinds of fighters.

---

[12] https://www.cdc.gov/nchs/products/databriefs/db244.htm, National Center for Health Statistics, Center of Disease Control, (Accessed February 2017)

[13] *Vision is the forward strategic plan that includes the desired goals and benchmarks of an organization's future.*

A) Preservationist – (Fighting for the Past). Fighting for the past is Preservation. These are the members who want things to stay as they used to be.
B) Conservationist – (Fighting for the Present). Fighting for the present is Conservation. These are the members who want things to stay as they are.
C) Futurist – (Fighting for the Future). Fighting for the future is Reservation. These are the members who want things to change.

CONGREGATIONS MATTER

A congregation is defined by Dr. Thomas C. Oden, in *Pastoral Theology: Essentials of Ministry* as "an assembly of persons brought together for common religious worship and affiliation." Dr. Oden further adds:

> "The Christian community is a covenant community bonded or kinship but by covenant community with God and spiritual relationship to Christ. Jesus regarded his disciples as sisters and brothers, the Christian community as a nurturing family, and the faithful as children of God. In a local congregation the pastor is called to encourage and guide this family in spirit, to care for each member and to wisely parent the process, seeking to help each member of the family of faith grow to fuller maturity."[14]

I view local Black churches as communities of people bonded together in covenant, nurtured as a family, and guided to care for one another. Most Black churches that I have attended and spoken in meet and exceed the definition of being a congregation through

---

[14] Thomas C. Oden, *Pastoral Theology: Essentials of Ministry* (New York, NY: HarperCollins, 1983), 188.

their historical legacy of seeking to help others to mature in the Christian faith.

LIFECYCLES OF CHURCHES

Every church goes through various lifecycles throughout its existence. According to Robert Dale, author of the book *To Dream Again:*

> "If a congregation doesn't take steps to open itself to revitalization, a plateau occurs. Decline begins. First people doubt the structures, next they doubt the goals, then they doubt the organization's basic beliefs, and finally they become completely alienated and drop out in total disillusionment."[15]

Dale outlines Five Stages of a Church's Life Cycle: Birth, Growth, Maturity, Decline, and Death. Whenever a church reaches the life cycle of decline there is an immediate need to initiate a renewal effort. A cursory definition of the word renewal is the intentional act of restoring or replenishing a thing. The act of "renewing" anything involves the process of restoration. However, renewing and restoring a congregation is not properly comparable to restoring an old painting or an antique car. There are more important questions to be answered in the pursuit of renewal such as "what makes a congregation alive?"

Thabiti Anyabwile, author of the book *Reviving the Black Church,* conveys the term renewal for a church and congregation as the incorporation of "new life." Anyabwile uses the biblical illustration of the Prophet Ezekiel's vision in Ezekiel Chapter 37. There the Prophetic voice called for the winds to blow upon the bones.[16] Anyabwile affirms that renewal is the breathing of new life into

---

[15] Robert D. Dale, *To Dream Again: How to Help Your Church Come Alive* (Eugene, OR: Wipf & Stock, 2004), 14.

[16] Thabiti M. Anyabwile, *Reviving the Black Church* (Tennessee: B&H Publishing, 2015), 9.

what it means to be Black and what it means to be Christian.[17] I envision congregational renewal as: a) a restoration of faithful attendance to regularly scheduled church services, prayer and Bible studies; b) a membership that is taught Christian doctrine from an African American perspective and is easily able to easily share their faith with others; and c) a networked community where there is mutual concern for one another, i.e., family, friends, neighbors, and acquaintances.

THE BLACK CHURCH AND ITS PASTOR

> Jeremiah 3:15 And I will give you pastors according to mine heart, which shall feed you with knowledge and understanding.

One of the most significant figures within a local Black church is its pastor. Churches are often judged to be "good" or "bad" based solely upon the community's perception of the pastor. He or she not only speaks as the voice of God, but also as the symbol of hope. Many Black churches have gained prominence simply because of their pastor's preaching style.

The Black pastor is a leader in all things related to Black people. Often, the pastor is called to resolve family, church, and community conflict without being properly informed of how deep the differences reside. He or she is usually the only therapist, counselor, advisor, and life-coach that many Black people will ever have. While some Black churches, for a variety of reasons, only see the pastor as a hireling that is sent to preach and to not get involved in the business or direction of the church itself; others see him or her as the lifeline. There is no simple way to quantify just how much is expected of the Black pastor. In a literal sense, the work of ministry within a Black community for the pastor can range from paying rent for a parishioner to attending a High School Graduation, making several

---

[17] Ibid., 9.

hospital visits, and returning multiple "crisis" phone calls all within the same day.

Within the Black church and culture there is a difference between pastoring a church and being a preacher. The church has traditionally licensed and ordained men and women as preachers, but these two certifications do not automatically transition a person into the pastoral ministry. Because formal education is not always required in most cases for Black congregations, there is not a uniform set of criteria in the selection of a pastor. The affect of not having a consistent means of qualifying preachers to become pastors has caused great distress in a lot of Black churches. Congregations have split into completely separate churches over personality differences related to the Black pastor.

Many Black congregations have been "preached" to for years and years, but very few congregations actually have a pastor with a shepherd's heart. The image of the Black pastor has changed and evolved over the years. Countless congregations have fallen victims to jack-legged preachers who were chasing women, money-hungry, and looking out for themselves. They fleeced the flocks and tarnished the image of what should have been the most respected and honest position in the community. The actions of a few con artists made it difficult for people to trust genuine pastors. Today's African American Pastor must be abreast of the times, intelligent, flexible, accountable, and still able to remain connected to the foundations of the past.

One of the main delivery styles of Black preaching involves "whooping" (singing or melodizing the message). "Whooping" remains very common in the Black church today. The Black Pastors of the past were usually illiterate but their "whooping" abilities were admired and embraced by congregations. Many of them were preaching messages that they had heard someone else preach. Sometimes they depended on a reader from the audience to read the scripture-text for them before they began expounding on its merits. A lot of them were Pastors of several churches at the same time and did not have the responsibility of teaching Bible Study or community involvement. In spite of the realities of their times, Black Pastors were still able to successfully preach the Gospel to their generation.

THE BLACK CHURCH AND SPIRITUAL CARE

Spiritual Care attends to a person's spiritual or religious needs as he or she copes with illness, loss, grief or pain; can help him or her heal emotionally as well as physically; and can help him or her rebuild relationships and regain a sense of spiritual wellbeing. Spiritual Care can also be described as the intentional operationalization of pastoral care functions (healing, guiding, liberating, sustaining, reconciling, nurturing, and providing empowering presence).[18] According to Dr. Edward Wimberly, "Caring within a local Black congregation is a response pattern to God's unfolding story in the midst. This unfolding story is one of liberation as well as healing, sustaining, guiding, and reconciling."[19] Dr. Wimberly's definition of Spiritual Care as a narrative is essential to the state of the Black church. "Storytelling is one style of pastoral care and counseling that takes place in the Black church. Not only is this style already used by pastors, it is a basic method used by Black people, both lay and clergy, to care for one another."[20]

The Black church has a long rich history of triumph over tragedy. In spite of its challenges, it continues to stand as the oldest institution within the Black Community because its people demonstrated care. It is my hope that our generation can find ways to strengthen the Black church and to aid in securing its future by providing healthy adequate Spiritual Care to all, especially those who feel excluded

---

[18] Pastoral Professionalism and Spiritual Care, *Course Syllabus*. (Accessed August, 2016)
[19] Edward P. Wimberly, *African American Pastoral Care* (Nashville, TN: Abingdon 2008), 18.
[20] Ibid., 2.

and disenfranchised by a discriminatory system. What would happen within the Black church if it focused on providing intentional Spiritual Care to the African American man? The possibilities would be endless.

CHAPTER 2

The Black Condition in America

MAAFA

The African Diaspora is the greatest atrocity in humanity's history. It is the most tragic, horrible, inhumane, degradation that the world has ever endured. Its impact is so devastating until centuries later the ripple affects are still being felt throughout the world. It has been called the Middle Passage, the European Slave Trade, the Transatlantic Slave Trade, and in most recent years the Triangular Atlantic Slave Trade; however, no description can adequately describe the horrors of this holocaust. The term "Maafa" which comes from the Kiswahili language means disaster, calamity, or catastrophe. It not only describes the historicity of the crimes against Black people, but it conveys the continued ongoing effects of these atrocities to this present day.[21] If there is any one word that might transcend language barriers and embrace part of the sufferings, pains and injustice of Black people, it is Maafa.

---

[21] William D. Wright, *Black History and Black Identity: A Call for a New Historiography,* (Westport, CT: Praeger, 2002), 117.

How can anyone justify the sin of slavery? How can anyone support the kidnapping, murdering, abusing, raping, molesting, and destroying of a people simply because of the color of their skin? How can anyone use the name of Jesus as the justification to bind, beat, and badger others who are made in the image of God and by their existence alone are redeemed by the same Lord? How can anyone subjugate children, emasculate men, and treat women of color like beast, while simultaneously embracing Christian tenants? How can anyone rationally and logically defend these actions with clean hands and a clear conscious? The answer is – no one. Although many White historians have tried to diminish the real atrocity of slavery and to justify the actions of plantation owners, slavery was and is a sin. According to Dr. L.H. Whelchel, Jr.:

> "The holocaust committed against African people during the period from the middle of the fifteenth century to the nineteenth century, did not occur simply because of an accident of geographical location, nor is the particular geometrical shape of the shipping routes of any essential importance. Both terms tend to obscure the historical reality of a consciously-planned enterprise ruthlessly carried out at the expense of a specific group of human beings."[22]

ERRONEOUS COMPARISONS

When the topic of American slavery is spoken of, many Caucasian people try to dismiss its horrors. Some have even tried to compare it to the biblical slavery of the Israelites or the indentured servitude status given to poor people of historical nations over centuries. Dr. Whelchel believes that these are nothing more than invalid attempts at diversions from the peculiar form of slavery practiced in

---

[22] L.K. Whelchel, Jr., *The History and Heritage of African American Churches* (St. Paul, MN: Paragon, 2011), 49-50.

the Americas. Rationalizers seek personal comfort with comments like, "everybody practiced slavery" or "Africans sold slaves too."[23] While it is true that almost every civilization has had some form of slavery, none of them practiced the type of institutionalized slavery as the Europeans did. Before the European slave trade began in 1440, most people who were slaves became so as the result of war.[24] Others became slaves as a result of unpaid debts and willful servitude through limited contracts. This form of slavery was known as indentured servitude.

In the Hebrew biblical text, God permitted His own people to become enslaved. Later, after their exodus from Egypt, they were allowed to have servants for seven years. At the end of seven years, all Hebrew servants and/or slaves owned by the people of the Lord were released. Arab Muslims, who were also extremely involved in the enslavement of African people, would often allow their slaves to be freed if they converted to the Islamic religion. It was only the European people, in contrast to all other cultures, that saw the benefits of perpetual free labor that turned slavery into a business. Hugh Thomas, author of *The Slave Trade: The Story of the Atlantic Slave Trade, 1440-1870*, estimates that 11 million Africans were transported to America.[25]

Many Presidents of the United States were slave owners and defenders of the wicked institution. John C. Calhoun, the seventh Vice-President of the United States argued that slavery was an act of God that allowed Christianity to be given to the heathen from across the ocean. In his 1837 speech in the United States Senate, Calhoun said, "never before has the black race of Central Africa, from the dawn of history to the present day, attained a condition so civilized and so improved, not only physically, but morally

---

[23] Whelchel, Jr., *The History and Heritage of African American Churches*, 50.
[24] Joy Degruy, *Post Traumatic Slave Syndrome* (Portland: Degruy Publications), 47.
[25] Hugh Thomas, *The Slave Trade: The Story of the Atlantic Slave Trade, 1440-1870* (New York: Touchstone), 804.

and intellectually."[26] Calhoun continues his speech by touting the improvements of Black people who were enslaved. He said, "it came to us in a low, degraded and savage condition, and in the course of a few generations it has grown into a comparatively civilized condition ... and general happiness is among the race." His words reflected a larger sentiment among most southern state slave owners of his day. By the romanticizing and sweetening up of the crimes that they were committing against Black people, they were able to distance their conscience from the possibility of any conviction.

RACE AND RACISM

Of greatest import, the American slavery experience was exclusively based on the notion of racial inferiority.[27] Many Caucasian with Eurocentric roots, which include vast numbers of White America, especially in the Old South operate off of one major premise, and from that one premise, all other beliefs are generated and governed. That one premise is racism. Racism differs from being a racist but one cannot be a racist without also strongly embracing racism. According to Dr. Neely Fuller, author of *The United Independent Compensatory Code/System/Concept – A Compensatory Counter-Racist Code*, racism is a global system that is also known as white supremacy and "if you don't understand racism – what it is and how it works – everything else that you do understand will only confuse you." In Fuller's assessment, a racist is any person who thinks, speaks, and acts to promote the practice of white supremacy (racism) at all times, in all places, and in all areas of people's activity.[28] A racist's ultimate objective is to establish, maintain, and expand the ideology of White Supremacy universally.

---

[26] John C. Calhoun, "Speech on the Reception of Abolition Petitions, Delivered in the Senate, February 6th, 1837," in Richard R. Cralle, ed., *Speeches of John C. Calhoun, Delivered in the House of Representatives and in the Senate of the United States* (New D. Appleton, 1853), 625-33.
[27] Degruy, *Post Traumatic Slave Syndrome*, 48.
[28] Neely Fuller, *The United Independent Compensatory Code/System/Concept A Compensatory Counter-Racist Code* (United States), 9.

Dr. Frances Cress Welsing, a Black Psychiatrist and lecturer expanding on the work of Dr. Neely Fuller adds: "all black people need to know what they are really facing and unless they understand it, they will be constantly trying to figure out – why is it that I can't move forward or get ahead." According to Dr. Fuller, the global system of racism is the reason why people of color (as a whole) are limited in their advancements on moving forward. He says that racism operates in all areas of people activities: Economics, Education, Entertainment, Labor, Law, Politics, Religion, Sex, and War.[29] Within every people activity, the equation of "white over non-white" is the driving force. In the event that a non-white begins to excel he or she threatens the erroneous belief that has been used to enslave, discriminate, exercise prejudice, and systematically subjugate all non-whites for thousands of years. Dr. Fuller adds in his book, "that erroneous teaching has been indoctrinated in the minds of many White people as the bedrock foundation for why they act as they do – and that teaching says Black people and people of color are genetically inferior and are incapable of functioning mentally or morally with whites."[30] The notion that white is right and black is wrong is not only a matter of the color of one's skin, but also a psychological state of mind in almost every Western culture. Carter G. Woodson explains:

> "The thought of inferiority of the Negro is drilled into him in almost every class he enters and in almost every book he studies. If he happens to leave school after he masters the fundamentals, before he finishes high school or reaches college, he will naturally escape some of this bias and may recover in time to be of service to his people."[31]

---

[29] Fuller, *The United Independent Compensatory Code/System/Concept A Compensatory Counter-Racist Code*, 1-3.
[30] Ibid. 8-15.
[31] Carter G. Woodson, *The Mis-Education of the Negro* (Chicago, IL: African American Images), 2.

POST TRAUMATIC SLAVE SYNDROME

We cannot fully understand the present conditioning of African Americans without thoroughly noting how slavery negatively impacted Black people emotionally, physically, and socially. American chattel slavery yielded stressors that were both disturbing and traumatic, exacting wound upon the African American psyche that continues to fester.[32] There is no complete way of knowing the full extent of the damage that has been done to Black people over the centuries. However, what is more obvious to visualize is the impact and resulting consequences that are directly linked to slavery and the centuries of terror that followed. Dr. Joy Degruy, author of *Post Traumatic Slave Syndrome America's Legacy Of Enduring Injury and Healing*, defines the condition as Post Traumatic Slave Syndrome (PTSS).

> Post Traumatic Slave Syndrome is a condition that exists when a population has experienced multigenerational trauma resulting from centuries of slavery and continues to experience oppression and institutionalized racism today. Added to this belief (real or imagined) that the benefits of the society in which they live are not accessible to them.[33]

Dr. Degruy, utilizing information taken from The Diagnostic Statistical Manual of Mental Disorders IV, Revised, lists seven emotional traumas that African American people were subjected to during slavery, Jim Crow and the continuation of prejudicial discrimination:

- A serious threat or harm to one's life or physical integrity.
- A threat or harm to one's children, spouse, or close relative.

---

[32] Degruy, *Post Traumatic Slave Syndrome*, 112.
[33] Ibid. 121.

- Sudden destruction of one's home or community.
- Seeing another person injured or killed as result of accident or physical violence.
- Learning about a serious threat to a relative or a close friend being kidnapped, tortured or killed.
- Stressor is experienced with intense fear, terror and helplessness.
- Stressor and disorder is considered to be more serious and will last longer when the stressor is of human design.[34]

Dr. Degruy has adequately described the Black condition in America. Post Traumatic Slave Syndrome is the result of behaviors that were brought about by specific circumstances that were intentionally laid upon the Black person. Unfortunately, both the behaviors and circumstances are immersed within every system of Western culture. It is seen in the industrialized prison system, the educational system, governmental systems and all other people-activity systems. Each system individually functions to serve and promote White advancement while allowing only a few Blacks to rise. Just as tributaries flow into a larger body of water, these stand-alone systems freely flow into the larger system of capitalism.

The capitalistic system that runs the economy of the United States and much of the world rewards those who have resources and punishes those who have not. Using Dr. Fuller's understanding of racism, many Black people have been systematically disenfranchised by the capitalistic system in every people-activity arena. Even Dr. Martin Luther King Jr. seemed to be keenly aware of the challenges that poor people would have when trying to fully participate within the system. The Poor People's Campaign became Dr. King's new initiative as he sought economic justice and fair opportunities for all. Whenever people develop a psyche of beliefs (real or imagined) that the benefits of the larger society will never be attained and are beyond reach, they are experiencing the real affect of racism. Black

---

[34] Ibid. 113-114.

people are often systematically left out of the capitalistic system's opportunities and are relegated to remain on the disadvantaged side of its equation.

BLACK POVERTY

Dr. King did not live long enough to realize the reality of financial freedom for all and sadly, no one else has been able to galvanize a sustainable movement to do so. The problem of PTSS permeates the Black condition and it is very prevalent in the area of Black economic development. Statistics show that 33 percent of Black Americans are stuck in poverty with no means of ever getting out of the cycle. In a 2018 published article titled, *The Inheritance of black poverty: It's all about the men* by Scott Winship, Richard Reeves, and Katherine Guyot, Black Americans born poor are much less likely to move up the income ladder than those in other racial groups, especially Whites. Many factors are at work, including educational inequalities, neighborhood effects, workplace discrimination, parenting, access to credit, rates of incarceration and so on.[35]

Professor of Sociology at the University of California, Dr. Melvin L. Oliver points out in his acclaimed book *Black Wealth/White Wealth* that while middle-class blacks now enjoy higher incomes, they "earn seventy cents for every dollar earned by middle-class whites but they possess only fifteen cents for every dollar of wealth held by middle-class whites."[36] His book supports the fact that despite a growing black middle class over the last 50 years, African Americans tend to lag in business development, a major source of wealth, as opposed to mere income. In essence, the majority of Black people lack the resources needed to create wealth.

---

[35] *Scott Winship is a former Brookings Institution fellow, now at the Joint Economic Committee.*

[36] Melvin Oliver, *Black Wealth/White Wealth* (New York: Routledge Taylor & Francis Group).

According to a 2000 Milken Institute[37] minority business report (prepared for the U.S. Commerce Department), blacks, while comprising 12.5 percent of the U.S. population, accounted for only 3.6 percent of businesses. Hispanics (who have become the largest minority since 2000) were 11 percent of the population, but accounted for 4.5 percent of businesses. Asian Americans who are 4 percent of the U.S. population and a third of the black population held 3.5 percent of businesses in the United States. Also according to the report, there were 1.4 million Latino-owned business, 1.1 million Asian and Native American businesses, but only 880,000 Black-owned enterprises. Annual revenue per business for Asian/Native American was $225,000; Hispanic, $130,000; and Blacks: $70,000. African Americans spend $600 to $700 billion as consumers but take in $91 billion in sales receipts as producers of products and services.

With these types of figures, it is easy to see why African Americans are having such a difficult time getting ahead. While some have managed to break the cycles of poverty, the vast majority, particularly those in very rural and also inner cities, are poor. President Lyndon Johnson, speaking at Howard University's 1965 Commencement states:

> Negro poverty is not white poverty. Many of its causes and many of its cures are the same. But there are differences – deep, corrosive, obstinate differences – radiating painful roots into the community, and into the family, and the nature of the individual. These differences are not racial differences. They are solely and simply the consequence of ancient brutality, past injustice, and present prejudice ...

---

[37] *A nonprofit, nonpartisan think tank determined to increase global prosperity by advancing collaborative solutions that widen access to capital, create jobs and improve health.*

For the Negro they are a constant reminder of oppression.[38]

President Johnson rightly distinguishes the differences between being White and poor from being Black and poor in America. He calls African American poverty a "consequence of ancient brutality, past injustice and present prejudice." Of these three factors (brutality, injustice and prejudice), President Johnson could have easily used one adjective – present. While some good-hearted White people would like to imagine that in ancient times or somewhere in the past, these bad things happened, in reality they still do. The consequences are more than a reminder of oppression they are also significantly displayed in PTSS.

In analyzing the consequences of systematic brutality, injustice, and prejudice, Dr. Degruy believes that a healthy self-esteem and an understanding of what something is worth is important for Black people to cope with PTSS. She equates a low estimation of value and an unhealthy self-esteem to the limited identity that many Blacks are confined to. Vacant esteem, being a symptom of PTSS, is transmitted from generation to generation through family, community, and society.[39] Through the transmission, undisciplined spending habits, misappropriation of finances, and disinterests in educational opportunities in higher learning institutions are always present.

BASIC ECONOMICS

Many Black people are unaware that there are four components of basic economics and production. These components are the driving force of the capitalistic system. Most Black people have heard these terms before but really do not know what they mean and how they

---

[38] Public Papers of the Presidents of the United States: Lyndon B. Johnson, 1965. Volume II, entry 301, pp. 635-640. Washington, D. C.: Government Printing Office, 1966.
[39] Degruy, *Post Traumatic Slave Syndrome*, 125.

affect them daily. The four major components are: Entrepreneurship, Capital, Labor, and Land.[40]

Capital is most commonly defined as accumulated wealth used to produce more wealth. It is also an asset or valuable instrument that can be used for exchange or service. In other words, capital is money. But it's not just money in the sense that Black poor people think of it. Capital is excess money as a resource. It is money that is left over when all the bills are paid and contributions have been made to savings. Excess money is the money that some people call "play" money. Play money is that which can be used for entertainment, hobbies, pleasure and investment. Capital is excess money that is available for discretionary spending.

For too long the Black church has been on both extremes of the subject of money. One extreme says that the love of money is the root of evil. However when we fail to teach people that "love' in this context is putting money ahead of God, we leave room for misunderstanding. To put it another way money is evil when we make it our god. Regrettably, the church has misled people into thinking that having money and owning great possessions are in some way evil. We can have money as long as money doesn't have us.

The other extreme says, "if we just confess it; money is coming to us and everyone can be rich." The prosperity gospel teaches that every Christian should be wealthy and healthy. In fact it promotes the idea that God wants us all to become millionaires and this is done by the act of exercising faith. This extreme is wrong too. We "can" have houses and cars and money, and become wealthy and some may even become millionaires; but this does not occur by just speaking it with our mouths. Faith without works is dead. It is the decisions that we make that can place us in a better position to get the most out of every dollar.

Since capital (excess money) is needed to produce more wealth,

---

[40] UKEssays. November 2018. Factors of production Land Labor Capital and Entrepreneur. [online]. Available from: https://www.ukessays.com/essays/business/four-factors-of-production-land-labor-capital-entrepreneur-business-essay.php?vref=1 [Accessed 4 March 2019].

if Black people are restricted, hindered and blocked from getting it, they will never become wealthy. The alternative for Blacks is to spend what they have because the possibility of acquiring capital is very minimal. Black families are large consumers of perishable items and very few have enough money saved to last 3 months.

Like everything else within a capitalistic system, there are multiple variables that determine the state of an individual. Generally, education, experience, and opportunity determine one's income. Unless a person is born with tremendous wealth, an income of some sort is needed. For Black people, the higher the income the better the chances become to acquire capital. Obtaining a higher income can be done vocationally by learning a trade, starting a business and employment. It can also be achieved academically by obtaining a degree in a field of study. The objective is the same no matter which route that is taken: increase income.

A second component of economics is labor. Labor is the same thing as work. Many Black people in the south were not afforded the opportunity to go to school during Jim Crow. Yet some were able to find employment, gained experience and worked their way through life without a formal education. In the 60's the United States government began to open jobs to minorities and women and many black people were able to gain federal and state employment. Labor is important in economics because without labor there is no production. Labor is also essential because it serves as a means to get capital.

A third component of economics is land. Some Black families were able to acquire land after the Civil War for farming. Those who were able to keep it during the harsh periods retained an invaluable asset. Land is a resource for agriculture, wildlife, and for building a home. When the Great Migration[41] occurred some Black people abandoned farms and land. For many, it was a grave mistake. Although land is used in reproduction, it is not reproduced. God

---

[41] *The period between 1916-1970 when African Americans moved from the South to West, Midwest and Northern cities in search of better economic opportunities.*

made all the land at one time and He has not made anymore. Black people left land that they owned to move into inner city apartments that would later be labeled as the projects. Land ownership is vital to Black economic development.

HATED WITHOUT A CAUSE

Along with economic and financial disparities, the condition of the African American is soaked with hatred by a world that sees color as an indication of intelligence, potential, value, and meaning. W.E.B. Du Bois not only confronts the challenge of being viewed by others as worthless but also how the African American sees him or herself. Du Bois calls this double-consciousness, the sense of always looking at one's self through the eyes of others.

> One ever feels his two-ness – an American, a Negro; two souls, two thoughts, two unreconciled strivings; two warring ideals in one dark body, whose dogged strength alone keeps it from being torn asunder.[42]

W.E. B. Du Bois correctly describes the reality of every Black person throughout any given day. African Americans are constantly viewed with suspicion or threat, followed or questioned in stores, unnecessarily pulled over by police and at times unfairly profiled for simply being in places where others do not think that they should. Dr. Fuller's assessment of the existence of racism in every people-activity is more than a notion it is the consciousness of duality within each Black person.

The white supremacy model and view of the world is most adequately described in Rudyard Kipling's 1899 poem, "The White Man's Burden." Kipling, speaking on behalf of the White race, embraces the belief that it is the White man's duty to civilize all

---

[42] W. E. B. Du Bois, The Souls of Black Folk (New York: Fine Creative Media, Inc.), 9.

non-white people of the earth by education and through erasing the normative beliefs of their cultures, traditions, and way of life. Herein lies the dilemma of African Americans – our true history has been stolen, erased or in some cases rewritten; our culture has been demonized as being barbaric; and we have been educated in a Euro-centric system that elevates white culture over every other.

The concept of race, as we presently understand it, is a relatively new development. Until European Imperialism sought to exploit the less fortunate, the world did not see color as a stigma or means of identity. Cultures, tribes, or nationality primarily identified the people of the world. Distinction was not made by the amount of melanin within bodies.[43] Although the concept of using race alone as the means of judgment is new, there seems to be little improvement in erasing and eradicating its deplorable affects. One does not need to look any further than the industrialized prison system in the United States to see its long lasting implications.

THE NEW JIM CROW

Immediately after Lincoln issued the Emancipation Proclamation on January 1, 1863, southern states began to undermine its intent by creating a new form of slavery. The Reconstruction Period provided hope and measures of relief, but it failed to adequately provide a safety net for Black people to transition into full participation within the larger society as equals. Michelle Alexander, author of *The New Jim Crow*, points out that Constitutional amendments guaranteeing African Americans "equal protection of the laws" and the right to vote proved as impotent as the Emancipation Proclamation once a White backlash against Reconstruction gained steam. Black people found themselves yet again powerless and relegated to convict leasing camps that were, in many cases, worse than slavery.[44]

Black people were herded into prison camps being charged

---

[43] Howard Winant, *The World Is a Ghetto: Race and Democracy Since World War II* (NY: Basic Books, 2001)
[44] Michelle Alexander, The New Jim Crow (New York: The New Press), 20.

with crimes that in almost every case were completely unfounded. Charges such as "insulting gestures, mischief, unauthorized assembly, and disorderly conduct" led to imprisonment. The outrage that most southerners had against Black people was intensified with harassment, whippings, and the ever-present threat of death through lynching, burning, drowning, and every conceivable horror known to mankind. A more viable alternative was to remove Black people from free society by imprisonment.

Legal incarceration became the favored method to control the newly freed Black person. Once a Black person was imprisoned, he or she lost most of their protections under the law and were able to be hired out by the state to work for plantation owners again for free. The hiring out of prisoners was called convict leasing. It was a new legal system of slavery that was sanctioned through the criminal justice system. Needless to say, Black men were incarcerated exponentially resulting in even more challenges for the Black family and community.

Although "convict leasing" is no longer in existence, the criminal justice system continues to incarcerate Black men at a much higher rate than any other people group. According to the National Association for the Advancement of Colored People (NAACP) between 1980 and 2015, the number of people incarcerated in America increased from roughly 500,000 to over 2.2 million. The Sentencing Project, an organization that works for fairness in the United States Criminal Justice System, confirms that Black men are nearly six times as likely to be incarcerated as White men and federal courts imposed prison sentences on Black men that were 19% longer than those imposed on similarly situated White men between 2011 and 2016.[45] People of color compose 37% of the United States population and disproportionately represent 67% of the prison population. According to Michelle Alexander, the mass incarceration of Black people is the New Jim Crow. Disguised as

---

[45] OpenInvest, *Who's in Prison in America?* 2/21/18 https://www.openinvest.co/blog/statistics-prison-america/ accessed January 2019.

the War on Drugs, maintaining law and order, or cracking down on crime, discrimination is perfectly legal and it is mainly based on a system of racism.

More Black men are imprisoned today than at any other moment in our nation's history.[46] The Black family does not have the presence of Black fathers anymore for a number reasons, but on top of the list is incarceration. The condition of Black people in America has never been ideal. So what does the current President of the United States Donald Trump and his supporters' mean when they say: "Make America Great Again?" Does that mean go back to slavery or Jim Crow? In the minds of most African Americans it is a call to arms for those who have deep-seated hatred for people of color. The Black condition suffers from PTSS but it has managed to survive and will continue to because of the strength of its people. Yet there is much work to be done within the Black community and this work begins with the reclamation of the identity and person of the Black man.

---

[46] Alexander, *The New Jim Crow*, 180.

CHAPTER 3

The Injured Black Man

THE PLACE MINISTRY SETTING

I am a pastor of an African American Church and have served as the primary Spiritual Care provider of the Pilgrim Rest Missionary Baptist Church of Brandon, Mississippi for approximately twenty years. My congregation is like most Black Churches all over the United States. The ratio of women to men is highly skewed. African American women greatly outnumber the men in every worship service and church event. There are some Sundays when the Adult Sunday School class for women is 6 times the attendance of the men's class. Black women also participate in other ministries, like the choir and praise team at a more consistent and faithful rate. In some cases, the women attending church have husbands and are in significant relationships; however as it relates to church attendance and participation, the men do not come with them. I began to ask myself: where are the Black men and why are they not coming to church?

PREVIOUS EFFORTS TO ADDRESS THIS MINISTRY ISSUE

"The process of secularization in Black communities has always meant a diminishing of the influence of religion and an erosion in the central importance of Black Churches.[47] The works of Lincoln and Mamiya sought to address the apparent erosion of the most cohesive and influential institution for Blacks that emerged from slavery – the Black Church. They note that there has been some "chipping away at the edges, particularly among un-churched underclass Black youth and some college educated, middle-class young adults."[48] Other scholars have sought to address the overall nuances in the African American experience of slavery, freedom, struggle, justice and equality and the role that the Black church has played in those involvements. W.E.B. Du Bois, Carter Woodson, Howard Thurman, James Cone, Cornel West, and a host of notable African American scholars have each contributed to conversations relating to the demise of the Black community – its people, culture, and spirituality (church). In conjunction with adequately addressing, analyzing, interpreting, and responding to the aftermath of the American chattel system of oppression, it is also essential to study one of the most misused and abused persons marginalized in the process – the Black man.

With the majority of Black congregations composed of mainly women, the likelihood of uniform growth among gender is greatly diminished. According to the Pew Research Forum, African American women are the highest populous of religious affiliation and significance.[49] The question becomes why are African American men no longer interested in attending Black churches? Jawanza Kunjufu outlines twenty-one reasons why most Black men do not

---

[47] C. Eric Lincoln and Lawrence H. Mamiya, *The Black Church in the African American Experience* (Durham: Duke University Press, 1990), 383.
[48] Lincoln and Mamiya, *The Black Church in the African American Experience*, 382.
[49] http://www.pewforum.org/2009/01/30/a-religious-portrait-of-african-americans/, A Religious Portrait of African Americans, (Accessed February 2017)

attend church. Two of his reasons are: 1) the lack of Christian role models and 2) the Black Church is too Eurocentric. Kunjufu gathered the data and literature through focus-group discussions and surveys. Regarding the lack of Christian role models for Black Men in a focus group of all Black Men, Kunjufu states:

> "Not one of them had a male that had been in their home who was saved and went to church. One brother said, "it should be obvious why we're here." Can you be anything that you have not seen? Can you be a Black man if you have not seen a Black man? Can you be a saved Black man if you haven't seen a [saved] Black man? If you haven't seen a Black man tithe, if you haven't seen a Black man in your house pray, it's going to be difficult if not impossible to emulate him."[50]

There is a systemic need to address the lack of Black men within Black churches because their vacancy is a large part of the spiritual and numerical decline in numbers.

THE BLACK MAN'S BURDEN

In Rudyard Kipling's 1899 poem titled "The White Man's Burden: The United States and The Philippine Islands," he urges the United States to carry the burden of civilizing third-world countries by spreading democracy and western culture to their lands. Many saw Kipling's poem as an effort to expand White colonialism across the globe. Although American democracy differed greatly from Great Britain's Empirical Colonial model, the end results for the native people of the land were the same. In response to Kipling's literary work, H.T. Johnson, a noted African American Minister responded with his own poem titled: "The Black Man's Burden."

---

[50] Jawanza Kunjufu, *Adam! Where Are You? Why Most Black Men Don't Go to Church* (Chicago: African American Images, 1997), 69-70.

> Pile on the Black Man's Burden.
> 'Tis nearest at your door;
> Why heed long bleeding Cuba,
> Or dark Hawaii's shore?
> Hail ye your fearless armies,
> Which menace feeble folks
> Who fight with clubs and arrows
> And brook your rifle's smoke.
> Pile on the Black Man's Burden
> His wail with laughter drown
> You've sealed the Red Man's problem,
> And will take up the Brown
> In vain ye seek to end it,
> With bullets, blood or death
> Better by far defend it
> With honor's holy breath.[51]

In 1976, when Ronald Reagan was running to gain the national Republican Presidential nomination, he famously labeled the Black man as a "strapping young buck." His words proved to serve as a uniting dog-whistle to those with an affinity to keep the Black man in his place. The idea of having to control and limit the freedom of Black men runs deeply within the veins of America. Thomas Jefferson, the noted father of American Democracy, sought to justify the inhumane treatment of Black men by attributing it to natural selection:

> His imagination is wild and extravagant, escapes incessantly from every restraint of reason and taste, and, in the course of it vagaries, leaves a tract of thought as incoherent and eccentric, as is the course of a meteor through the sky... we are compelled to

---

[51] H.T. Johnson, "The Black Man's Burden," *Voice of Missions*, VII (Atlanta: April 1899), 1. Reprinted in Willard B. Gatewood, Jr., *Black Americans and the White Man's Burden, 1898–1903* (Urbana: University of Illinois Press), 1975, 183–184.

enroll him at the bottom of the column... nature has been less bountiful to them in the endowments of the head.[52]

What is the root cause of such hatred and hostility towards the Black man? How can anyone be so indoctrinated until they believe that all Black men are only wild and vagrant "strapping bucks" possessing no restraint of reason and taste? The unfortunate answer lies primarily with the historical white Christian church and its leaders. Ronald Reagan and Thomas Jefferson's beliefs were not uncommon among certain White groups and might have been formulated in the false biblical teaching that being Black is a curse. More specifically, Blackness and all of its Afrocentric features are the result of Ham's curse.

DISPELLING THE MYTHICAL CURSE OF HAM

> Genesis 9:18 And the sons of Noah, that went forth of the ark, were Shem, and Ham, and Japheth: and Ham is the father of Canaan. [19] These are the three sons of Noah: and of them was the whole earth overspread. [20] And Noah began to be an husbandman, and he planted a vineyard: [21] And he drank of the wine, and was drunken; and he was uncovered within his tent. [22] And Ham, the father of Canaan, saw the nakedness of his father, and told his two brethren without. [23] And Shem and Japheth took a garment, and laid it upon both their shoulders, and went backward, and covered the nakedness of their father; and their faces were backward, and they saw not their father's nakedness.

---

[52] Thomas Jefferson, Notes on the State of Virginia, chapter 14 (Paris: 1785), http://xroads.virginia.edu/~hyper/JEFFERSON/ch14.html.

[24] And Noah awoke from his wine, and knew what his younger son had done unto him. [25] And he said, Cursed be Canaan; a servant of servants shall he be unto his brethren. [26] And he said, Blessed be the LORD God of Shem; and Canaan shall be his servant. [27] God shall enlarge Japheth, and he shall dwell in the tents of Shem; and Canaan shall be his servant.

Within this text lies one of the most misused, misrepresented, and misunderstood occurrences, as it relates to the Black man, in all of Scripture. The narrative of Noah's story is one of epic proportion. The God of the universe commissioned him to build an ark for the perpetuation of human and zoological life. Judgment was pronounced over the earth and a flood ensued that completely destroyed all human beings and animals that were not aboard the ark. Noah, his wife, his three sons - Shem, Ham, and Japheth - and their wives, along with the animals that were taken aboard and remained on the ark for approximately 375 days. After the floodwaters subsided, the story of righteousness and triumph over evil takes a drastic turn downward.

According to Genesis 10:6, Noah's son Ham is the father of Cush (Ethiopia), Mizraim (Egypt), Phut (Libya), and Canaan. Almost every serious and honest scholar agrees that all of the descendants of Ham are people of color. It is worth noting that Ham has four sons all together and only one has a curse pronounced over him. The other three sons, that are also Black, are not involved nor attached to the so-called curse of Ham.

After everyone exited the ark, Noah became a farmer and planted a vineyard and made wine. One day while he was drunk, he lied down naked and uncovered in his tent. Ham, the father of Canaan, saw the nakedness of Noah and told his two brothers Shem and Japheth. Shem and Japheth took a garment and walked in backwards to cover the nakedness of their father, Noah. They had their faces turned away so as to not see their father exposed. When

Noah awoke from his wine and learned what Ham had done, he pronounced a curse.

> "Cursed be Canaan; a servant of servants he shall be to his brethren... Blessed be the Lord, God of Shem, and Canaan shall be his servant. God shall enlarge Japheth, and he shall dwell in the tents of Shem; and Canaan shall be his servant."

What is most remarkable about this text is that Ham, the son who saw his father naked, is not mentioned at all. There is no curse issued upon Ham by God or by Noah. In fact, Noah is the one who issued the curse on Canaan; God did not. Why isn't it called the curse of Canaan instead of the curse of Ham? Remember, Ham has four sons and they are all Black; none of the other three sons are mentioned in this text. In an effort to justify the enslavement of Black people, many historical White scholars have erroneously labeled the event as the curse of Ham in an effort to say that all Black people are cursed. It must also be noted that nowhere within the text is there any mentioning of skin color. These same scholars taught that the curse of Ham involved a change in skin color, intellectual aptitude, hair texture, and body features. The text does not endorse any of these racial tones, nor does it state that Black people are genetically inferior to White people.

WHERE ARE THE BLACK MEN?

According to official estimates from the United States Census Bureau, the Black male population in the United States was 21.5 million in 2013. These numbers translate into 48% of the total Black populous in America. It is difficult to believe that there are in excess of 20 million Black men in the United States, partly because they are visibly absent. If any reasonable Black person is asked, "Where are the Black men?" a familiar list will soon ensue. The answers are usually, "they are in prison, in jail, dead, in a gang, on drugs, selling drugs, homosexual, unemployed, living with his mother, staying with some woman or I have no idea." The search for the Black man should not be so hard, especially since they make up 48% of the entire complexity of African American people.

It seems like everybody is looking for the Black male. Black women are looking for a good Black man to marry. Black children, especially Black boys, are looking for Black men to nurture them and give them a sense of direction. Schools are looking for dedicated and consistent African American men to volunteer for role model and rites of passage programs. The Black church is also looking for African American men.[53]

Is there really a shortage of Black men? According to Jawanza Kunjufu, we lose more African American males than females at birth. He confirms that there are 1,965 deaths per 100,000 live births for Black boys versus 1,603 per 100,000 deaths for Black girls. Out of the starting blocks, the male shortage begins at birth with 362 fewer Black males.[54] Simple reasoning will conclude that if there are not sufficient Black male children, there will not be an adequate amount of Black male adults. Whether by design or by default, it is catastrophic to have an insufficient number of Black males for the Black community.

There are two biblical examples of the deliberate gender genocide of males. King Pharaoh ordered the killing of all Hebrew boys in Exodus 1:15-22 and King Herod massacred all males under the age of 2 years in St. Matthew 2:16-18. In both biblical narratives, a male child was being birthed to provide deliverance for the people. Although African American male children are not being exterminated at birth, 362 fewer males may result in 362 fewer

---

[53] Kunjufu, *Adam! Where Are You?*, 4.
[54] Ibid., 39.

men. Of these fewer men, how many might have been physicians, inventors, or leaders?

The Centers for Disease Control and Prevention ranks "Unintentional Injuries" as the leading cause of death in African American males between the ages of 1-14 years old.[55] When these numbers are compounded with homicide, which is the leading cause of death among Black men between the ages of 15-34, and medical neglect among middle-aged Black men, the perception of a shortage greatly increases. With one in three Black men being incarcerated throughout their lifetime, and hundreds of thousands more not being able to find gainful employment, the state of the Black man is perplexing. Although the statement once cited by President Obama that "more Black men are in prison than are in college" is no longer true, the effects of its original authenticity remain. There may not be an actual numerical shortage of Black men, but there certainly is a shortage of available, educated, healthy, working, un-incarcerated Black men in America.

WHY SOME BLACK MEN DON'T GO TO CHURCH

Dr. Howard Thurman's philosophy regarding the condition of Black people from a Christian perspective is essential to trying to grapple with why some Black men don't attend church. Dr. Thurman connects the ontology of Christ to those who have been systematically disenfranchised.

> "The masses of men live with their backs constantly against the wall. They are the poor, the disinherited, the dispossessed. What does our religion say to them? The issue in not what it counsels them to do for others whose need may be greater, but what religion offers to meet their own needs. The search

---

[55] https://www.cdc.gov/healthequity/lcod/men/2011/LCODBlackmales2011.pdf

for an answer to this question is perhaps the most important religious quest of modern life."[56]

According to Dr. Thurman, religion must offer something that is tangible to those who have nothing. It must not only recognize their plight, but it must give specific answers to plaguing problems. Since all men are searching for meaning, the Black man must find meaning in his suffering, and that explanation cannot simply be a myriad of clichés and glossy religious overtones. The Black church has often soothed its parishioner's agony and pains by speaking of a better world to come. The sweet by and by was the place where the injurious wrongs, imposed upon their very being, would be made right. There, the wicked would cease from troubling, and the weary would be at rest. When what religion offers does not give help in the here and present, it will not be taken seriously. After all, how could it be that every other people group could readily enjoy freedom and prosperity now, while Black people would have to wait to see Jesus to get their fair share?

In Dr. Kunjufu's book entitled: *Adam! Where Are You?*, he lists 21 reasons as causes why Black men do not attend church.

(1) Hypocrisy – Many Black men believe that there is too much contradiction between what was being said in church and what was being done in the community.
(2) Ego/Dictatorial – Many Black men were irritated about always being told what the Pastor said about this and what the Pastor said about that.
(3) Faith-Submission-Trust-Forgiveness-Angry At God – Many Black men struggled with fully understanding these concepts and how they translated into their lives.
(4) Passivity – Many Black men can't reconcile the idea of walking away from injustice with the right to stand up for one's self.

---

[56] Howard Thurman, *Jesus and the Disinherited* (Boston: Beacon Press, 1996), 13.

(5) Tithing – Many Black men do not understand how giving 10% to the church is actually giving to God.

(6) Irrelevance – Many Black men believe the church has failed to address many of the issues within the community such as crime, drugs, teen pregnancy, lack of recreational opportunities, unemployment, and single parenting.

(7) Eurocentric – Many Black men see the image of a white, blonde, blue-eyed image of Jesus as an image to be worshipped as sacrilegious.

(8) Length of Service – Many Black men believe that church worship services are too long.

(9) Too Emotional – Many Black men see praise, singing, dancing, and shouting as only emotional displays and unnecessary.

(10) Sports – Many Black men see Sundays as a day to relax and watch sporting games on television.

(11) Attire/Dress Code – Many Black men do not have a large selection of church clothes.

(12) Classism/Unemployment – Many Black men feel embarrassed by not having money to put in the offering plate.

(13) Education – Many Black men are afraid of being asked to read out loud.

(14) Sexuality and Drugs – Many Black men believe that the church intrudes too much into their personal affairs.

(15) Homosexuality – Many Black men believe that the church is made up of women, elders, children, and homosexuals.

(16) Spirituality/Worshiping Alone/Universalism – Many Black men embrace spirituality but do not see how it relates to church.

(17) Heaven – Many Black men do not like the idea of having to wait to die to have peace and enjoyment.

(18) Evangelism – Many Black men have never been properly witnessed to.

(19) Lack of Christian Role Models – Many Black men do not have another significant Black man of which to model.

(20) Streets/Peer Pressure – Many Black men feel more comfortable among their peers or simply prefer to be left alone.

(21) Parental Double-Standard Forces When A Child – Many Black men say that there was preferential treatment of other siblings when they were children.

While some of these reasons may seem trivial, the residual affect translates into the absence of Black men in Black churches.

A NEW APPROACH

A new strategy must be established that intentionally addresses the issues specific to the Black man. All Spiritual Care, education and formation within the Black church must also include resources to highlight, uplift and resource Black Men. The model must also have as its primary goal the deliberate and intentional outreach to bring Black Men back to church. As stated by Jawanza Kunjufu: "there is a disproportionate ratio of females to males in the church, when figures reach this magnitude, we have to find reasons why African American men have strayed away from church and what can be done to bring them back."[57]

Because the African American is suffering from an identity crisis further complicated by three hundred years of slavery and one hundred years of segregation, the negative impact continues to plague the minds and hearts of Black men. The psychological affects of Post Traumatic Slave Syndrome must be met with the provision of sufficient Spiritual Care from Black churches that provides healing for the Black man.

---

[57] Kunjufu, *Adam! Where Are You?, 129.*

CHAPTER 4

The Healing of the Black Man

Hebrews 11:1 Now faith is the substance of things hoped for, the evidence of things not seen.

CHOOSING TO HOPE

Perhaps there is no better message that can be given to the Black man than the message of hope. Embedded within the message of hope is the dream of a day when all injustices will end. Hope is what has given Black people the courage to stand and overcome the terrible, sinful, and shameful disgrace of slavery and the ungodly continuation of segregation and prejudice. Black people have continued to have hope, long before our Nation's first Black President Barak Obama used it to propel himself into the Oval Office. It was hope that kept our Black ancestors believing and praying for a better day for their children. Their hopes were realized even though they never lived to see it. Hope is an interesting word because it implies that what a person desires can actually be attained. It suggests that events can turn from the worst to the better. It is therefore hope that keeps the Black man's faith intact.

Dr. Barbara Fredrickson, a Principal Investigator of the Positive Emotions and Psychophysiology Lab and Professor at the University of North Carolina defines hope in this way:

> "Hope comes into play when our circumstances are dire, when things are not well, or when at least there's uncertainty about how things will turn out. Hope opens up and removes the binders of fear and despair by allowing us to see the big picture and also to become creative in establishing a better future."[58]

Within Dr. Fredrickson's definition of hope is what I believe is the methodology of healing for the Black man. According to her definition:

(1) We don't have the type of life we wished for because we weren't as creative as we should have been.
(2) We weren't as creative as we should have been because we didn't see the big picture.
(3) We didn't see the big picture because we let despair become dominant in our thinking.
(4) We let despair become dominant in our thinking because we were afraid of the binders that were either put on us by others or put on us by ourselves.

HOPE VS. HOPELESSNESS

The unfortunate negative consequences of the sequence outlined by Dr. Fredrickson may lead to a false hope; causing Black men to become dependent upon someone else to do for them what they should actually do for themselves. The psychological damage of

---

[58] Fredrickson, Barbara L., et al. (2008). "Open Hearts Build Lives: Positive Emotions, Induced Through Loving-Kindness Meditation, Build Consequential Personal Resources" (PDF). *Journal of Personality and Social Psychology, 95*, pp. 1045–1062. Retrieved 2012-10-02.

slavery is real and it left the Black man with Post Traumatic Slave Syndrome. However, it also placed him in a unique position of hopelessness. This unique form of hopelessness is what is wrong with a lot of Black men in our nation right now. In order to begin the process of healing, there must be a better understanding, not only of what hope *means* but also of what hope *does*. For Hope is not just wishing that things will change; instead, it is taking the next step in becoming creative in making those changes come to pass.

> Hope says:
> "Help me by showing me how to help myself"
> Hopelessness says:
> "Just help me"
> Hope says:
> "Teach me so that I can teach others"
> Hopelessness says:
> "If you know how I don't have to know how"
> Hope says:
> "Pick me up so that I can pick others up"
> Hopelessness says:
> "Just pick me up"
> Hope says:
> "If you let me try it, I can do it"
> Hopelessness says:
> "You do it for me"
> Hope says:
> "Get me started and I'll finish"
> Hopelessness says:
> "When you finish yours, finish mine"

A false sense of hope is in the Black community at large and is more readily seen in the Black man. The issues are bigger than the church, because the church is secondary to the home, and in many cases now, it is secondary to all other established institutions. Yet, somehow a mentality of "unhealthy dependence" has been created within many Black men. This mentality has Black men expecting others to "give" them things that they have not earned. Sometimes it says: "since you can do this for me, I'm expecting you to do it." In other words "my issue is your problem." These sayings are just a few indicators that reveal hopelessness.

Those who are hopeless are in need of healing because, at its core, hopelessness is a frame of mind. In most cases, hopeless people are dependent on those who have hope and sometimes their dependence can become overwhelming. A hopeless person can drain, deplete, and consume every ounce of hope within a relationship, community, family, and even the church.

LET THE HEALING BEGIN

One of the steps that must be taken towards the healing of the Black man begins internally. Since hopelessness is a frame of mind that is often shaped by one's surroundings and experience, the mind has to become creative. Within each Black man is an untapped wealth of creativity. He built pyramids thousands of years ago that remain to this day. He civilized ancient cultures by providing mathematics, science, religion, astronomy, philosophy, and medicine. The Egyptian culture laid the foundation for Greece and later Rome. The world revolves around the thoughts and minds of the ancient Black man's creativity. The Black man must become creative again and begin to utilize his complete God-given mind as he once did. To be creative also means to image and do it. Anything in the mind can be formed and made with our hands.

The healing of the Black man by necessity must include engaging his imagination. African American men will renew lost hope as they recapture creativity and construct something that will last longer than their lifetime. This means that his healing is also in construction (building). The Black man has to build his way out of hopelessness. The same mind that imagined the Sphinx in Egypt, built that Sphinx. When given the right tools, time and resources, the Black man can build a better future for himself and his family.

Again, using Dr. Barbara Fredrickson's, definition of Hope,

Black men have the potential to set the trajectory for a new world. Dr. Fredrickson says: "hope comes into play when our circumstances are dire, when things are not well, or when at least there's uncertainty about how things will turn out." She adds: "hope opens up and removes the binders of fear and despair by allowing us to see the big picture and also to become creative in establishing a better future." As we use this well thought-out definition of hope for the healing of the Black man, the mission becomes the application of its truths.

THE CYCLE OF HOPELESSNESS

By Dr. Fredrickson's definition, the worst damage in the world that can be done to us is the damage that we do to ourselves when we lose hope. The issue related to the Black man is that he has seemingly developed a mindset of hopelessness that keeps him in a cycle of despair. According to the Institute of Clinical Mental and Emotional Support, a cycle of hopelessness can emerge through a series of detrimental occurrences.

First, bad decisions are made that cause a sense of anxiety and worry. As one begins to worry, he or she realizes that the damages, results, and consequences of those bad decisions are beyond their ability to fix. Sometimes those decisions are socially related, as in living beyond one's means. At other times they involve love conflicts associated with an unhealthy marriage or stress from a dead-end job. Anxiety can originate from any area in life that creates unhealthy stress; these areas are generally where a person is incapable of changing their condition.

The cycle continues when there are a multitude of broken things that a person is unable to fix. When a host of "broken things" surround a person, their environment becomes one of dysfunction. As one tries to function within an environment that is surrounded by dysfunctional things, a sense of hopelessness slowly sets in. When there is no apparent way to come out of the dysfunctional situation, bad habits can form. These harmful habits serve to further trap a person into the cycle of dysfunction. Even though things are not working, out of some form of fear or in an effort to impress others or hide the truth, some people remain in the dysfunctional loop. The longer a person tries to function within the dilemma, ironically, the better he or she becomes at managing a dysfunctional state. Habits are formed around all things being dysfunctional and a mindset is eventually established.

THE MINDSET OF HOPELESSNESS

A mindset is a state of mind that is set and determined. It is one of the most difficult parts of a person to change. When a mind is set, it directly accepts its own conclusions as the only truth. Sadly, creativity is hindered when we cannot see beyond where we were or where we are. If we are facing despair and dire circumstances that is not the time to stop being creative but it is a time to create a new vision for our future. That vision must come from God.

The prayer of the Apostle Paul in Ephesians 1:18 desires "that the eyes of our understanding become enlightened." In other words the Black man has to begin to see what God has planned for him. Vision is needed when there is a wide gap between what is and what could be. People with vision end up where their hope leads them and those with no vision end up stuck in the cycle of hopelessness.

A few years ago I served as a mentor at a local middle school. When I arrived one day, the assistant principal informed me that two young ladies were in her office for fighting. I was there to mentor young boys, not girls, but the administrator asked me to help. After I talked with them, I found out that they were fighting over a young boy. These two girls were about to be expelled from school over a boy – he of whom was already seeing another girl. I found out later that these two girls were related to each other and something similar had happened with both of their moms. The cycle of hopelessness with their mothers had begun its revolution within these children.

AROUND AND AROUND WE GO

In order for the Black man to be healed, the cycle of hopelessness that he is trapped in must be broken. The word cycle is defined as "a set of events that reoccur without change, the completion of a set leaves circumstances unchanged except for the passage of time." In other words, a person goes all the way around the circle and when they get back to where they started, the only thing that has changed is the amount of time that it took to travel around the circle. Does this describe Black life in America? Does this describe what is happening with our Black children? Does this describe what has happened to the Black man? In many ways it does. It is a cycle; because the set of events that are occurring have already happened before and nothing is changing but the people involved and the time it takes to start the next revolution.

Another word for a cycle is a "pattern." What is within the grandparents shows up within the parents and what is within the parents appears within the children. What is within the children will eventually show up within the grandchildren and so on and so forth. This was the case with the two young girls at the school. They simply repeated what their mothers had done.

Some might say that there is no correlation between my behavior and my child's. "I never did or even thought of some of the things that these children are doing today." Yes, that may be true, but remember; you probably did things your parents never thought of or did too – so the cycle continues. Others may say: "Yes. But where my children are, I have never been before and they are nothing like I was." This may also be true. However, if we asked your parents; they would probably say the same thing about you. You were nothing like them in any shape, form, or fashion either, yet the cycle continues. The specifics and particulars may differ but the end result is the same.

To put it another way, our grandparents "walked" around the circle. Our parents "jogged" around the circle. You and I "ran" around the circle, and our children are "driving" around the circle. The only difference is the people involved and the passage of time that it takes to get around the same circle. Our grandparents did it at age 46; our parents did it at age 36; we did it at age 26; and your children are doing it at age 16. What is the difference? The difference is the people involved and the time. The end result is still the same and we are right back where we started. The cycle continues. There are several cycles that are affecting the African American community at large but specifically the Black man.

The Black man, in some cases, is trapped in the poverty cycle. The poverty rate for Black households (according to the U.S. Census Bureau) is 27.2%.[59] Another cycle is the teenage pregnancy cycle. According to the Guttmacher Institute September Report: "for young women between the ages of 15-19, black teens are most likely to become pregnant (134 per 1000)."[60] The majority of the Black girls are getting pregnant by Black boys who are not financially able to care for a child.

The Black man also has to deal with the cycle of unemployment. According to Generation Opportunity, a conservative nonprofit organization advocating for economic opportunity for young adults, the unemployment rate for African Americans between the ages of 18-29 is 24.2 percent. Out of this number, "over half of those seeking employment are unemployable for the positions of which they are seeking to find jobs. Many of them are unemployable because of past criminal records, or simply not having sufficient education to meet the minimum requirements of those positions."[61] Then there's the cycle of education or the lack of education. Black men are the least educated of all people groups in America. As all of these cycles continue to revolve, it is apparent that the Black man needs to be healed.

LET THE HEALING CONTINUE

Each generation is tasked with creating a better future for their children. Our forefathers did so, and we must do the same. Every

---

[59] https://www.census.gov/topics/income-poverty/poverty.html
[60] https://www.guttmacher.org/report/us-adolescent-pregnancy-trends-2013 Pregnancies, Births and Abortions Among Adolescents and Young Women in the United States, 2013: National and State Trends by Age, Race and Ethnicity
[61] *Generation Opportunity advances policy change, holds policymakers accountable, fights for opportunity, and defends the freedoms of young Americans.*

Black man has something to contribute, but he must get involved. What kind of future do *you* want? The answer to this question can be found in a myriad of complexities. If we asked it agriculturally, the farmer would say, "We want a future where hunger and starvation are gone." If we asked the educator, they would say, "We want a world were no child is left behind." If we asked the philosopher, the professor would say, "We want a world filled with thinkers." If we asked the politician, the Republicans and Democrats would say, "We want a world that supports our ideology." But if we asked the Black man, what would he say? He would say, *"I want a future world that is no longer injurious to my state of being and has provided me to space to be completely healed."*

Dr. Fredrickson's definition states: "hope opens up and removes the binders of fear and despair by allowing us to see the big picture and also to become creative in establishing a better future." Within her definition, there are three words that serve to heal the Black man: 1) *creative* 2) *better* 3) *future*. These three words are distinct in their on rite, but when combined together we are forced to face the reality that a better future does not happen on its own. An improved future is created by those who really want it and are willing to exercise hope to obtain it.

The healing process for the Black man requires affirmative action. In this case I am not referring to the legal Affirmative Action that gives Black people a chance to advance. I am more directly speaking of actions that feed into our ambitions of creativity. In other words, the Black man will know where he is going by what he is doing creatively. The healing is within the intentional effort of each Black man to create a better future by using everything within him self and every available resource at his disposal.

CHAPTER 5

Forming the F.A.C.E.-I.T. Fellowship

> Proverbs 27:19 As in water face answereth to face, so the heart of man to man.

The F.A.C.E.-I.T. (Finding Answers Concerning Every Issue Today) Fellowship was founded in 2017. For over a decade, I hosted an annual Men's Conference on the Saturday before Father's Day. The Men's Conference has centered upon the spiritual, natural, and overall development of Black men. At the close of our Men's Conference on June 17, 2017, the Pastors in attendance felt led of the Holy Spirit and agreed that we needed to continue the "Fellowship" and move it from church to church. In the summer of 2017, I met with several of the Pastors as a focus group to further solidify our mission and work. Their valuable insights and godly counsel created a platform for dialogue and action. We moved forward with God's grace and held our first official F.A.C.E.-I.T. Fellowship Meeting in September of 2017.

The F.A.C.E.-I.T. Fellowship is a model that represents a new approach to addressing the unfortunately consistent hemorrhaging within African American churches. It does so by strategically ministering to Black Men and providing spiritual formation and renewal. The Fellowship seeks to "Reclaim the Black Man and his Family," by deliberately and intentionally addressing the issues that he faces on a daily basis. Its purpose is to completely uplift each Black man by empowering, resourcing, and edifying him through the Word of God. By doing so, he will become a better person, husband, father, church member, and community asset for the kingdom of God.

The F.A.C.E.-I.T. Fellowship is comprised of Pastors, religious leaders, community activist, and Black men of every walk of life, working together in partnership to learn and receive the Gospel of Jesus Christ in an authentic and uplifting way. Each Pastor serves within the leadership of the Seven Areas of the Fellowship's Ministry listed below.

(1) Black Men and Black Youth Mentoring
(2) Prison Ministry and Re-Entry Programs
(3) Church Staff and Laity Development and Resourcing
(4) Pastor and Spouse Support System
(5) Black Men Empowerment and Community Involvement
(6) Associate Minister Development and Resourcing
(7) Food Pantry, Meals-on-Wheels and Health Fairs

The cornerstone of the F.A.C.E.-I.T. Fellowship is its dialogue within the monthly meetings. These sessions are specifically designed to facilitate listening, to assimilate narratives from Black men, and to offer alternate ways to look at life from a biblical Christian perspective. One of the objectives of each session is to engage Black men by getting them to tell and listen to each other's personal story of life. Their stories and experiences as a Black man set the stage for a larger narrative and provide a means to introduce biblical concepts regarding the development of spiritual character and spirituality.

THE NARRATIVE PEDAGOGY

The tools of listening and dialogue are essential to how each session flows. Although local Pastors serve as facilitators and discussion guides, no real hierarchical structure exists within the sessions. Every attender must employ the tool of listening because each story has something useful to all. In the process of storytelling, essential points of emphasis may be stressed that can allow for in-depth discussions after the narration. Every session is also designed to allow for linking and sharing similarities. When others have similar stories or experiences, a comradeship between them is possible. The overall idea is to establish harmony through similarities with the hopes that Black men will discover that they all share the same struggles and challenges respectively. A new community of unity can emerge through this discovery.

F.A.C.E.–I.T. FELLOWSHIP SESSIONS

Each F.A.C.E.–I.T. Fellowship session begins by introducing a wholesome character trait from the Bible as an instrument of learning. A facilitating Pastor teaches a brief lesson about the character trait from the Bible. Handouts, PowerPoint Presentations, visual learning objects, and resource tools are used to assist the Pastor in communicating the lesson to the listeners. The Pastor is encouraged to end each lesson by sharing a personal story in which the character trait used in the lesson was employed in his life. Black men are then asked to share their stories that are related to the character trait in the lesson. A discussion of similarities or differences within each person's story follows as linking is established. After the character lesson, story-sharing and story-linking process, a panel of Pastors field questions regarding the character trait lesson or any other issue that is on the minds of attenders. There are learning tasks associated with each facet of the curriculum to assist as evaluation indicators.

<u>Phase 1: Biblically-based Character Lesson</u> – 15 minutes

Learning Task: Teaching of a character trait located within the Bible that is relevant to the Black man's daily life.

Learning (What is to be learned?) - What the Bible says concerning this character trait either directly through a biblical personality or indirectly through concepts, ideologies, and ideas.

Transfer (What is to be gained?) - How can utilizing this character trait help to make the individual a better person and thereby become a better husband, father, friend, church member, community member, etc.

Impact (What is to be done?) – Look for opportunities to employ this character trait privately and publically by sharing it and its benefits with others.

Phase 2: Story Telling - 15 minutes

Learning Task: Share and listen to life stories of Black men related to the biblically based character trait lesson.

Learning - Black men will listen to one another's story regarding the character trait.

Transfer - Black men are encouraged to relate information from their own personal experience.

Impact - Each Black man will gain a greater understanding of each other and begin to build relationships.

Whoever wants to share a story related to the character trait in the lesson will be given the opportunity. The telling of the story should focus primarily upon the character trait to ensure that the discussion remains consistent.

Phase 3: Story Linking – 15 minutes

Learning Task: Assimilating similar themes from everyone's stories.

Learning – Gaining insights from another person's perspective.

Transfer – Relating the newly gained insights to current or future life events.

Impact – Pondering and sharing new insights with others who may be in similar situations.

After each participant tells individual stories, the ensuing discussion may include the reason why certain choices were made throughout the experience. Others may need clarity or advice in further discussion.

Phase 4: Panel Discussion –15 minutes

Learning Task: Identifying scenarios where this character trait is useful.

Learning – Finding realistic ways to consistently utilize this character trait.

Transfer – Seeking others to share the benefits of operating with this character trait.

Impact – Having a sense of collectively implementing and operating with this trait as a community.

F.A.C.E.-I.T. SESSION CHARACTER TRAIT LESSON EXAMPLE

Character Lesson Title: Man Up!

> Jeremiah 5:1 Run ye to and fro through the streets of Jerusalem, and see now, and know, and seek in the broad places thereof, if ye can find a man, if

there be any that executeth judgment, that seeketh the truth; and I will pardon it.

Where do we begin? How does a Black man, "Man Up?" Where is the starting point? What is the first step? We begin the work of "Manning Up" by being Intentional.

#1 Being Intentional – To be intentional is to intend on doing what is good.

> Psalms 34:14 Depart from evil, and do good; seek peace, and pursue it.

Doing "good" is a reflection on what is in a man's heart. It is the "action" of good. A man must put what is in his heart into action. This includes: giving, sharing, communicating, and caring. What do you care about? Who do you care about? Did you know that if you care about something or someone, it is very natural for you to "take care" of them? In your own life, whatever you don't care about is not taken care of. If you don't care about your lawn the grass will not be groomed. If you don't care about your car you won't wash it and keep the inside clean. If you don't care about your wife you won't communicate or share with her (you may do what you are required to do, but you won't do anything extra).

In order to "Man Up" we must be intentional by doing good to one another and caring about our brothers. The next step is to "Be Relational."

#2 – Be Relational – To be relational is to have friendships with people who can hold us accountable.

> Proverbs 27:6 He that shows himself friendly will have friends; but the kisses of an enemy are deceitful.

A friend can help us with things that nobody else can by being honest and truthful. Friends may also be required to hurt us at times with the truth about ourselves. Yet real friends will not simply point out our flaws and faults but they will encourage us through them. They are not trying to "fix" us because no one is capable of adequately repairing, healing, managing, changing, and helping a person but God.

In order to "Man Up" we must be relational by earning the right to speak at a deeper level into the lives of our friends. The next step is to "Be Available."

#3 – Be Available – To be available is to purposefully make time to participate and be involved.

> St. Luke 14:16 Then said he unto him, A certain man made a great supper, and bade many: [17] And sent his servant at supper time to say to them that were bidden, Come; for all things are now ready. [18] And they all with one consent began to make excuse. The first said unto him, I have bought a piece of ground, and I must needs go and see it: I pray thee have me excused. [19] And another said, I have bought five yoke of oxen, and I go to prove them: I pray thee have me excused. [20] And another said, I have married a wife, and therefore I cannot come.

The parable addressed in St. Luke 14:16-20 points to the unavailability of each man. The first man's excuse dealt with real estate. He had purchased a piece of property without even looking at it or having it surveyed. Obviously, this makes no sense because no person in his or her right mind would purchase real estate without examining it first. The second man's excuse seems even more far-fetched because it includes buying animals that have not been proven. His excuse would be the equivalence of one of us buying a truck without test-driving it first. The final man's excuse was related to his social life. He used his wife as his excuse for being unavailable.

In order to "Man Up" we must be available and stop making excuses with the things we own, desire, or enjoy.

Jeremiah was "looking" for a man. Why? Because no man was volunteering and no man could be found. The kind of man that Jeremiah was looking for is you. God will bless others by you. God will forgive others by you. God will save others by you. God will lift others by you. God will restore others by you. Let us all look for ways to be more intentional, relational, and available.

STORY TELLING ASPECT OF MAN UP!

Over the years that I have served as a local Pastor, I have encountered hundreds of people at different junctures in their faith journey. Although no two individuals are the same, there are certain similarities that we all share. Each of us has social, physical, emotional, and spiritual desires and needs that help to formulate who we are and who we hope to become.

A few years ago, I encountered an elderly gentleman who was living in squalor conditions. In fact, he was living out of his car at a service station. Although I had known of the gentleman all of my life, I did not have any social relationship with him. I wanted to help him as best I could, but I really did not know how.

I started going to the service station often to get gasoline, to talk with him, and to bring him food and snacks. Over a period of several weeks, I established a working relationship with him. Through our conversations, I discovered that he had family members that lived a few towns away. After researching names and contacts, I finally contacted one of his siblings and told her of her brother's living conditions. Together, she and I were able to find a place for him to stay that was near her home.

When I shared the news with him that his family wanted him to move into a home near them, he was very reluctant and embarrassed to face them. I assured him that I would go with him to ensure that everything went well and to give him an opportunity to reconnect. After only a few days, he was comfortable enough to move into the home that was provided and to reestablish relationships with his family that were once broken.

Throughout the experience with the elderly gentleman, I had to be intentional, relational and available in many ways. I spent money, gave my time, and deliberately got involved. I learned a lot about him as we became friends, but I discovered a lot more about myself than I knew before.

- Are there any examples where you had to be deliberately intentional with others?
- Do you have any examples of events in your life when you were deliberately relational with others?
- Can you think of times in your life when you became deliberately available for others?

Dr. Ava S. Harvey, Sr.

POWERPOINT HANDOUT
ASPECT OF MAN UP!

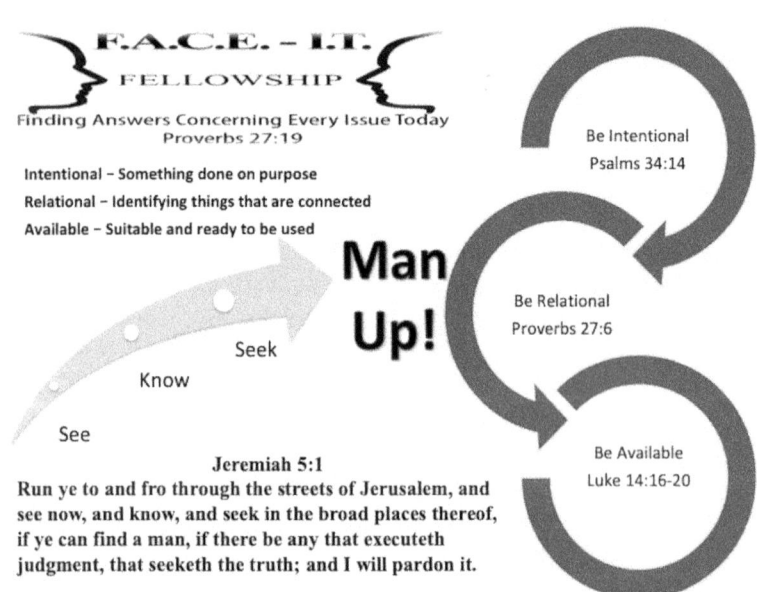

Jeremiah 5:1
Run ye to and fro through the streets of Jerusalem, and see now, and know, and seek in the broad places thereof, if ye can find a man, if there be any that executeth judgment, that seeketh the truth; and I will pardon it.

STORY LINKING ASPECT OF MAN UP!

During the story linking aspect of each F.A.C.E.–I.T. session, attendees will be encouraged to share their story related to the character traits of the lesson. The purpose of story linking is for others to gain insightful information for personal use. The newly gained insights may be used in making decisions regarding current or future life events.

PANEL DISCUSSION OF MAN UP!

During the panel discussion aspect of each F.A.C.E.–I.T. session, attendees will be asked to participate in open discussion of the topic. The panel will help to guide the discussion by identifying scenarios where the character traits in the lessons may be usefully applied.

MINISTRY PLAN TO SUPPORT BLACK CHURCHES

Participation with F.A.C.E.–I.T. is completely voluntary. All churches, regardless of denominational affiliation are welcomed to participate in the monthly sessions and the annual conference. There are no fees, membership commitments, or affiliation ties with F.A.C.E.–I.T. that will hinder or interfere with any previous church-related associations or denominations.

The F.A.C.E.–I.T. Model is significant because it can be utilized in maintaining and enriching Spiritual Care within numerically and spiritually declining African American Churches. Those who wish to reach and resource Black men within the church and community can also utilize the model in their areas. This new model gives space for Black men's voices to be heard both individually and collectively. Not only does it promote recognition of Black men, it also gives the much-needed respect to those who have been overlooked, suppressed and systematically disenfranchised. With this model, the Black church can be restored to the pinnacle of each community and serve as the beacon of light for African American men in this dim world.

CHAPTER 6

The F.A.C.E.-I.T. Curriculum

When I began the F.A.C.E.-I.T. Curriculum with the Black men of the church where I serve as the pastor, I selected a day and time of fellowship that would be most convenient for the majority of the brothers. Fortunately, the same day of the week and time is currently being used for the combined fellowship with churches. The Black men of my church and I envisioned the construction of a Spiritual Character Wall (SCW). The wall is comprised of bricks and is designed in a manner consistent with that of a standard masonry wall. Embedded within each brick is a character topic that we have thoroughly discussed, studied, and agreed to allow its placement. Our men's wall is located in the foyer area of our church where it is clearly and visibly seen each time someone enters the area.

There are innumerable character traits within the Old and New Testaments of the Bible. Our local church brotherhood was able to successfully complete over 35 within a five-year period, before formulating the combined fellowship. I am including ten F.A.C.E.-I.T. Character Lessons within this chapter that are a part of the larger curriculum. Each F.A.C.E.-I.T. lesson highlights a specific characteristic to serve as the topic of discussion and the narrative of the meeting. These character traits are desired of all Black men and – through the process of story-linking with other brothers, pastoral advice from godly leaders, and freedom to discuss challenges – an atmosphere of healing is generated.

CHARACTER TRAIT LESSON ONE
Development by Doing
(See figure 6.1)

Colossians 3:23 And whatsoever ye do, do it heartily, as to the Lord, and not unto men.

Doing is the act of performing something. It is the execution of an act. The end result of doing is accomplishment/achievement or failure. There are four ways to look at the noun of "doing" and every Black man must seek to become a "Doer" in these areas.

1. Proactive – acting in anticipation of future needs and changes. Ecclesiastes 11:6.
2. Reactive – responding to needs and changes that have already occurred. St. Luke 10:30-36.
3. Inactive – being idle and not responding to needs and changes. Proverbs 20:4.
4. Coactive – responding to needs and changes together with others. St. Matthew 18:19 -20.

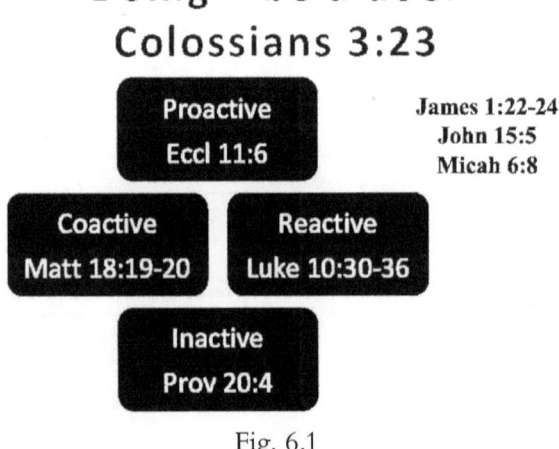

Fig. 6.1

CHARACTER TRAIT LESSON TWO
Developing Reliability
(See figure 6.2)

Colossians 1:10 That ye might walk worthy of the Lord unto all pleasing, being fruitful in every good work, and increasing in the knowledge of God.

Dependability is being reliable. It is a value trait that exhibits the reliability of a person to others. It is displayed in integrity, truthfulness, and consistency. Every Black man should develop the qualities of being dependable.

Dependability has two factors of consistency:

1. Availability – able to be counted, present and ready for immediate use.
2. Reliability – able to be counted on; consistency with confidence.

Dependability can be thought of as being composed of three elements:

A) Attributes - A way to assess dependability.
B) Threats - An understanding of the things that can affect dependability.
C) Means - Ways to increase dependability.

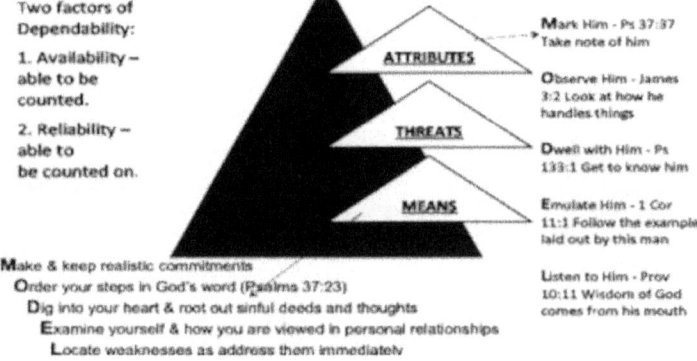

Fig. 6.2

CHARACTER TRAIT LESSON THREE
Developing Honor
(See figure 6.3)

Romans 12:10 Be kindly affectioned one to another with brotherly love; in honour preferring one another.

To Honor something is to put value upon it. It is to respect with dignity and uphold it as important. Honor is something that we "give" by choice. The opposite of honor is dishonor. It means to treat something as common, ordinary, and of little or no value. Honor is important to the brotherhood of Black men because it helps to align our respect for each other.

There are several people that the Bible says we are told to Honor:

- The bible teaches us to Honor God from a sincere heart. Honoring God is giving God the glory by showing sincere praise and worship.
- We are commanded to Honor our Parents. Honoring our parents is showing sincere appreciation.
- We are expected to Honor our Wives: We honor our wives by showing her sincere love.
- We are told to Honor all men and the king (our Leaders). Honoring all men (brothers) is showing sincere respect.
- We are to Honor our Spiritual Leaders, the Pastors, Elders, and Leaders of the flocks.

There are several enemies that are out to destroy honor:

Selfishness – putting your needs, desires, cares, and wants before others.

Insincerity – being hypocritical by going through the motions without sincerity.

Neglect – being careless and detached from responsibilities.

Becoming an Honorable Man happens in stages. Similar to a child developing into adulthood, God develops us into honorable Black men.

1. Enforced Obedience – When we are forced to obey. The first authority in our lives was likely our parents or guardians and they made us obey them.
2. Willful Obedience – When we obey without being forced to do so. This happens as we begin to understand the consequences of our actions.
3. Mutual Obedience – When we obey out of love. At this point we are not afraid of consequences anymore and we love and honor the ones who led us into truth.

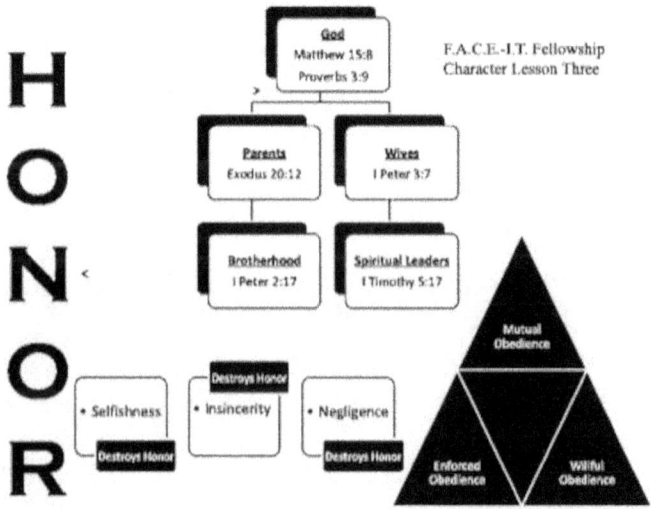

Fig. 6.3

CHARACTER TRAIT LESSON FOUR
Developing Discernment
(See figure 6.4)

Hebrews 5:14 But strong meat belongeth to them that are of full age, even those who by reason of use have their senses exercised to discern both good and evil.

Discernment is the ability to comprehend and evaluate clearly. It means that one can see the true nature of things. Discernment does not only come from God; but it can also come from human intuition and perception. As we grow in experience, our ability to discern usually grows stronger, providing us with insight that propels us toward greater wisdom. The fellowship needs Black men with discernment.

Discernment is developed in three ways:

1. Stop – (Ezekiel 44:23): We have to first stop what we are doing to get an understanding of what is right & wrong. Our conscious can be so seared until we are confused as to what is right & wrong. There are a number of things that we must also stop: lying, playing, tripping, and being unstable.
2. Stoop – (St. John 8:3-8): The act of stooping is the process of bending forward and lowering yourself down. Stooping is one of the postures of prayer, but it is also a symbol of humility.
3. Stand – (Malachi 3:18): It is time for Black men to stand up and show the world that we are a unique and precious people. We must take a stand for righteousness in our homes, churches and communities.

The exercise of discernment occurs through the process of testing and proving (I Thessalonians 5:21, Acts 17:11, and I John 4:1).

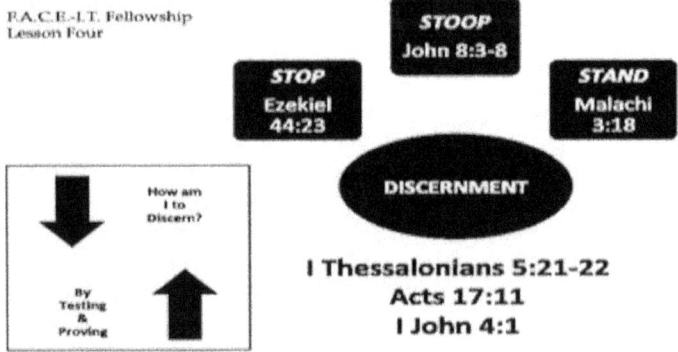

Fig. 6.4

CHARACTER TRAIT LESSON FIVE
Developing Loyalty
(See figure 6.5)

1 Samuel 18:1-4

Loyalty is faithfulness and devotion to a person, country, group or cause. In our times, loyalty is a virtue that is becoming rare between Black men. Loyalty must become a major part of our fellowship. It starts with our willingness to make personal sacrifices to strengthen our relationships. Loyalty is our covenant.

One of the most powerful examples of loyalty in Scripture is the friendship and covenant that Jonathan made with David.

There are 5 things about the loyalty of Jonathan & David found in I Samuel 18:1-4

1. Their souls were knit together. When something is knit it is cross-stitched together and interlaced. This represents oneness of spirit. It's the same thing that Jesus does to our spirit.
2. Outer garments were exchanged. Jesus exchanged His robes for ours.
3. Jonathan gave David his sword. Since a sword is a weapon of defense, we must protect each other and our covenant.
4. Jonathan gave David his bow. The bow is a weapon of distance. When we see things that are far away that may endanger our covenant, we will remove them.
5. Belts were exchanged. The belts symbolize inner strength. We vow to strengthen each other.

Dr. Ava S. Harvey, Sr.

THE FELLOWSHIP "WE WILLS" OF LOYALTY

We will serve God through Christ
We will serve our families
We will serve our churches in the right spirit
We will encourage others in hard times
We will be committed to excellence
We will point out the good in others
We will fortify healthy relationships

Spiritual Connection
(Knit Souls)

Appearance Changed
(Clothes Given)

Mutual Protection
(Sword Given)

Future Protection
(Bow Given)

Mutual Strength
(Belt Given)

Pastor Ava S. Harvey, Sr.

F.A.C.E.-I.T. Fellowship Lesson Five

Fig. 6.5

CHARACTER TRAIT LESSON SIX
Developing Righteousness
(See figure 6.6)

Righteousness – Becoming and Being A Righteous Man

> Ezekiel 22:30 And I sought for a man among them, that should make up the hedge, and stand in the gap before me for the land, that I should not destroy it: but I found none.

Righteous is defined as being upright, moral, straight, and filled with justice, integrity, honesty and goodwill. Righteousness is a character quality that reflects an individual's heart. Our desire is to develop the right attitude regarding righteousness. Most of us pride ourselves in always being right. It is our internal nature and ego at work that pushes us to be right about almost everything. Our efforts need to be channeled towards a different kind of righteousness that does not include selfishness or pride. Some how we have mixed up righteousness with always being right. Being right does not always mean that we are righteous and neither does being righteous mean that we are always right.

Steps towards the "Right" Righteousness

Step One:
1. Justification – Where God makes us right with him. (Romans 5:1 and I Corinthians 6:9-11)

Step Two:
2. Consecration - Where we work on our imperfections, ways, weaknesses, and tendencies as a continual act of Sanctification. (II Corinthians 6:17-18 and Romans 8:12-13)

Step Three:
3. Continuation – Where we cultivate a "craving" for the things of the Lord and eat at His table. (Job 23:12 and I Peter 2:1-3)

Becoming a righteous man happens as we become pure in heart.

1. Pray for it: Psalms 51:10
2. Apply your heart to the Word: Proverbs 22:17
3. Guide your heart in the right way: Proverbs 23:19
4. Draw nigh to God: Hebrews 10:22
5. Love God with your whole heart: St. Luke 10:27

Righteousness – Becoming a Righteous Man

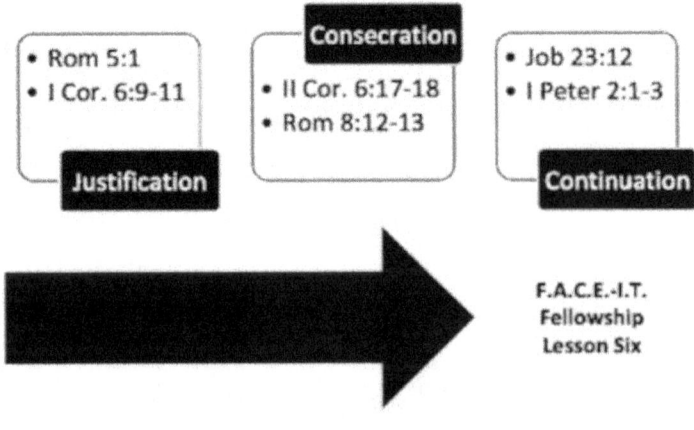

Fig. 6.6

CHARACTER TRAIT LESSON SEVEN
Developing Availability
(See figure 6.7)

St. Luke 14:16 Then said he unto him, A certain man made a great supper, and bade many: [17] And sent his servant at supper time to say to them that were bidden, Come; for all things are now ready. [18] And they all with one consent began to make excuse. The first said unto him, I have bought a piece of ground, and I must needs go and see it: I pray thee have me excused. [19] And another said, I have bought five yoke of oxen, and I go to prove them: I pray thee have me excused. [20] And another said, I have married a wife, and therefore I cannot come.

Availability:

1. Present and ready for use; at hand; accessible:
2. Capable of being obtained; obtainable:
3. Qualified and willing to serve or assist:

I remember applying for my first part time job. The interview was very brief but when we got to the end, they asked me "What hours would I be available?" I was in high school so I knew that I was not available anytime during school hours. During basketball season I had practice after school each day, so my availability was only after school, after basketball season and on the weekends.

When I finished my 1st degree in college I interviewed with a company for employment. In the interview they asked me, "Are you available to travel?" As I matriculated in corporate America, it was very common to be asked, "Are you available to travel and to be on call?" What the interviewers were getting at - and they do this with everybody – was, "How much of your time, skill, and professionalism can we expect out of you to do this job?"

Time is like money in a sense because it is spent frequently. It can be saved, shared, used wisely, or misused. Time is one of the most valuable and precious commodities that God gives us. It is up to us to make ourselves available for what matters most.

We can tell how important things are to us by how much time we spend with them.

There are 168 hours in a week, and for the average adult:

- 40 to 60 hours a week are usually spent on a job (including going to and from)
- 50 to 60 hours a week are spent sleeping
- 25 to 30 hours are spent watching television, on the internet, or with hobbies

This leaves about 20 hours a week for spouses, children, and personal spiritual development.

God wants availability from each of us but there are always hindrances.

3 major hindrances to our availability:

I. My Property

> St. Luke 14:18 And they all with one consent began to make excuse. The first said unto him, I have bought a piece of ground, and I must needs go and see it: I pray thee have me excused.

Our property is the place we reside, our house. When our house is more important than God's house, we will not be available.

II. My Possessions

> St. Luke 14:19 And another said, I have bought five yoke of oxen, and I go to prove them: I pray thee have me excused.

The things that I possess can possess me.

III. My Passions

> St. Luke 14:20 And another said, I have married a wife, and therefore I cannot come.

Our wives are important, but they are not before the Lord. Any passion we have must be governed to keep order. If a man cannot govern his passions, he will self-destruct.

Are you available? God wants to use us. And when we become available, our property, possessions, and passions should come with it.

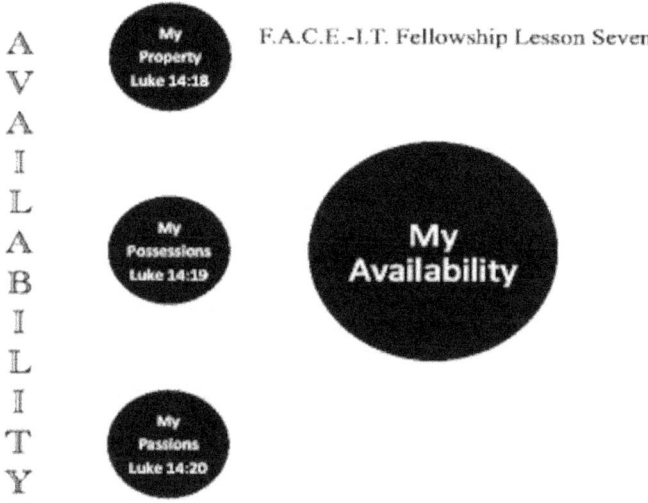

Fig. 6.7

CHARACTER TRAIT LESSON EIGHT
Developing Devotion – Becoming Devout
(See figure 6.8)

Being devout is having earnest sincerity of devotion and loyalty to a purpose and cause. It involves being committed to God, family, church, and the community. To be devout is to be dedicated, stable, sold-out and all-in with every part of you (spirit, soul, and body). It is to be "given" over to a movement until it is more than just a part of you; it becomes you. It's what you stand for, work for, and live for.

God is looking for devout Black men of standard, stability, and security. Our families, churches, and communities need strong Black devout men to be the head of their wife and the father of their children. We need devout Black men in our fellowship.

> St. Luke 2:25 And, behold, there was a man in Jerusalem, whose name was Simeon; and the same man was just and devout, waiting for the consolation of Israel: and the Holy Ghost was upon him.

1. "There was a man in Jerusalem": The first thing we see about a devout man is where he is. He is in the City of God - God's headquarters on earth, where the temple is, and where true worship is.
2. "Whose name was Simeon": The second thing we see is about a devout man is who he is. His name has two different meanings, one that hears God and/or one that God hears. In other words, if he speaks God hears him. And if God speaks he hears God. This is the essence of communication.
3. "The same man was just and devout": The third thing we see is his character. He is just and devout. He is dedicated, sold-out, all-in, given over, totally committed, and loyal. We get the picture of a stable, solid, faithful, secure, and balanced man.

4. "Waiting for the consolation of Israel": The fourth thing we see is what the man is doing. He is waiting on the consolation of Israel. Consolation comes from the word "console", which means to relieve one's disappointment, burden and grief. He is waiting on the Lord to move a burden off the people.
5. "And the Holy Ghost was upon him": The fifth thing we see is what was upon him. The Holy Ghost was upon this man empowering him for service.

From this lesson we have 3 applications about being a devout man:

- A devout man is dedicated – Acts 8:2
- A devout man is detectable – Acts 22:12 (Paul's testimony)
- A devout man draws others – Acts 2:5

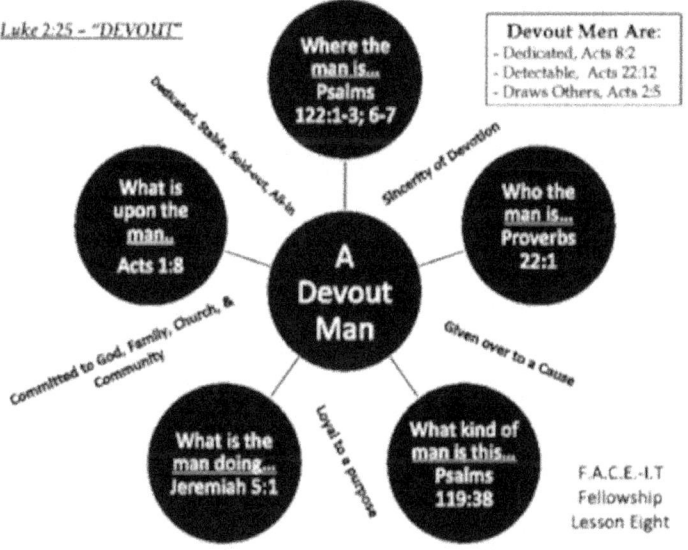

Fig. 6.8

CHARACTER TRAIT LESSON NINE
Developing Prudence
(See figure 6.9)

Prudence is a word not used too often in our vocabulary but it is really a good word because it deals with using common sense and thinking things through. Operating with prudence is the ability to govern and discipline oneself using reason, being skillful in the management of affairs, and having good judgment in the use of resources. Prudence is one of the main aspects of wisdom.

There are 6 areas where we need to exercise prudence.

1. Prudent people know that everybody doesn't need to know everything (Proverbs 12:16).

    The idea behind this proverb is that prudent people are able to keep from reacting hastily or harshly to insults or mistreatment.

2. Prudent people give cautious answers (Proverbs 12:23).

    The meaning here is that a prudent person does not tell everything they know. It's better to have something to say and say nothing than to have nothing to say and say something useless.

3. Prudent people think ahead (Proverbs 22:3).

    It is easy sometimes to confuse faith with foolishness. Jesus told us not to worry about tomorrow, but nowhere does He command us not to plan for tomorrow. In fact, being a good steward of the time God gives us implies that we must prepare the best we can for life's eventualities. Prudent people think ahead, and do what they can to prepare for the future.

4. Prudent people use discernment (Proverbs 14:15).

   Prudent people don't believe everything they hear. They learn to listen with discernment and separate what is true from what is false. They are attentive and keenly aware.

5. Prudent people handle correction well (Proverbs 15:5).

   When others try to offer correction or make suggestions about our behavior and habits, we should keep an open mind. Prudent people are not too proud to accept criticism and use it to make themselves better people.

6. Prudent people study (Proverbs 18:15)

   Prudent people never stop learning and growing.

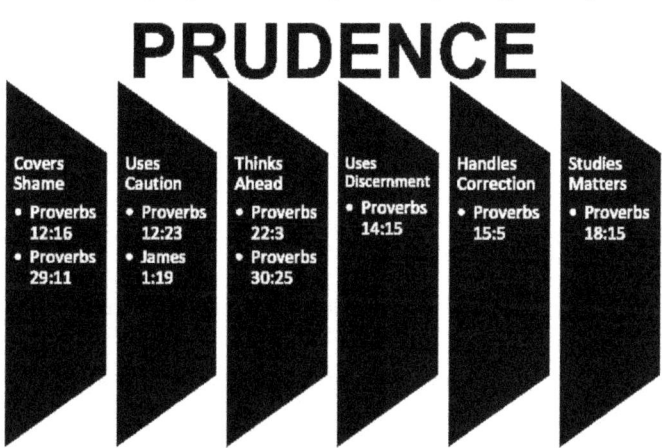

Fig. 6.9

CHARACTER TRAIT LESSON TEN
Developing Consistency
(See figure 6.10)

Consistency is defined as having steadfast adherence to the same principles, course and form. It is to "stay the course" and remain true to the mission. Consistency is being able to do the same thing again and again and again. It's the repetitive nature and example that makes others come to continually expect the same level and flow. Consistency is having the same personality regularly until it becomes who you are to others.

Consistency is needed in the fellowship. We cannot have a strong brotherhood of Black men without consistency.

Therefore let us become more consistent in our:

1. Ways – (Proverbs 16:7) Our ways are our mannerism.
2. Personality – (Romans 12:18) Our personality is the visible quality that other people see in us.
3. Thoughts – (Proverbs 23:7) We are who we think and we become what we think.
4. Actions/Deeds – (Colossians 3:17) Our actions should be consistent with a person who is a believer in Christ.

Consistency requires Four Keys:

Involvement – We must be a part of what the Lord is doing (Galatians 6:4).

Interest – We must have a real desire to be a doer (James 1:22).

Integrity – We must operate within the Word and Will of God (Psalms 86:11).

Identification – We must know who we are in the Lord (2 Corinthians 5:17).

FACE-IT Finding Answers Concerning Every Issue Today

It's time to become consistent. Can we count on you?

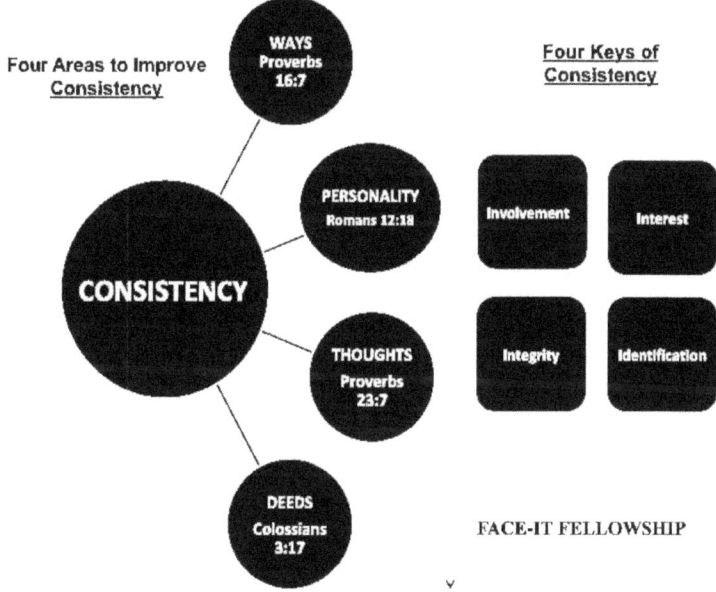

Fig. 6.10

THE VISION FORWARD

The F.A.C.E.-I.T. Fellowship Model has been implemented in central Mississippi and the results have been very positive. For nearly two years, the fellowship has met consistently and discussed topics ranging from pornography, infidelity, financial concerns, lack of self-esteem and identity complexes as well as matters related to social concerns with fatherlessness and abuse. In June 2018, the first F.A.C.E.-I.T. Fellowship Conference was enacted. The conference generated an attendance of over 1400 people over a two-night span with high numbers of African American male participants. A greater awareness of issues that concern Black men has been highlighted and elevated into a new position of prominence.

Since the formation of the FACE-IT Fellowship and Conference, there has been an increase in Black male participation within the connected churches. A genuine camaraderie has also been established between the pastors and congregations of each church that will hopefully continue in the years to come.

BIBLIOGRAPHY

Anyabwile, Thabiti M. *The Decline of African American Theology: From Biblical Faith to Cultural Captivity*. Illinois: InterVarsity Press, 2007.

Barnett, Ned. "New Pastors, Small Churches." *Faith and Leadership* (February 14, 2011), https://www.faithandleadership.com/features/articles/new-pastors-small-churches (accessed September 20, 2017).

Bradley, Anthony B. *Liberating Black Theology: The Bible and the Black Experience in America*. Illinois: Crossway Books, 2010.

Cone, James H. *A Black Theology and Black Power*. New York: Seabury Press, 1969.

Cone, James H. *A Black Theology of Liberation*. New York: Orbis Books, 2010.

Cone, James H. *God of the Oppressed*. New York: Seabury Press, 1997.

Degruy, Joy. *Post Traumatic Slave Syndrome*. Portland: Joy DeGruy Publications Inc., 2005.

Du Bois, W.E.B. *The Souls of Black Folks*. New York: Barnes & Noble Books, 2003.

Foster, Richard J. *Celebration of Discipline*. NY: HarperCollins, 1998.

Franklin, Robert, Michael Dash and Stephen Rasor, "ITC/ FaithFactor Project 2000," *Interdenominational Theological Center,* 2000.

Frazier, E. Franklin. *The Negro Church in America.* New York: Schocken Books, 1974.

Fredrickson, Barbara L. *"Open Hearts Build Lives: Positive Emotions, Induced Through Loving-Kindness Meditation, Build Consequential Personal Resources."* Journal of Personality and Social Psychology, 2008.

https://www.census.gov/topics/income-poverty/poverty.html

https://www.guttmacher.org/report/us-adolescent-pregnancy-trends-2013 *(Pregnancies, Births and Abortions Among Adolescents and Young Women in the United States, 2013: National and State Trends by Age, Race and Ethnicity).*

https://www.ukessays.com/essays/business/four-factors-of-production-land-labor-capital-entrepreneur-business-essay.php?vref=1 [Accessed 4 March 2019]. *UKEssays. November 2018. Factors of production Land Labor Capital and Entrepreneur.*

Hugh, Thomas. *The Slave Trade: The Story of the Atlantic Slave Trade, 1440-1870.* New York: Touchstone, 1997.

Kunjufu, Jawanza. Adam! *Where Are You? Why Most Black Men Don't Go to Church.* Chicago: African American Images, 1997.

Lincoln, C. Eric and Lawrence H. Mamiya. *The Black Church in the African American Experience.* Durham: Duke University Press. 1990.

Moore, Thorn. "The African American Church: A Source of Empowerment." *Prevention in Human Services* 10.1300/J293v10n01_09 (October 13, 2008) https://www.researchgate.net/publication/254381982_The_African-American_Church (accessed January 19, 2017).

"National Center for Health Statistics." Centers for Disease Control and Prevention. Accessed April 2017. https://www.cdc.gov/nchs/products/databriefs/db244.htm.

Oden, Thomas C. *Pastoral Theology: Essentials of Ministry.* New York: HarperCollins Publishers, 1983.

Paris, Peter J. *The Social Teaching of the Black Churches.* Philadelphia: Fortress Press, 1985.

Pew Research Center. "The Generations Defined." The Millennials (Born: 1981-1997), Generation X (Born: 1965-1980) Baby Boomer Generation (Born: 1946-1964), Silent Generation (Born: 1928-1945), Greatest Generation (Born: Before 1928) http://assets.pewresearch.org/wp-content/uploads/sites/12/2015/01/FT_generations-defined.png (accessed April 2017)

Pinn, Anthony B. *Understanding and Transforming the Black Church.* Eugene: Cascade Books, 2010.

Slaughter, F. Keith. *Therapeutic Dimensions of Black Preaching.* USA: Get-Success Publishing, 2014.

Thurman, Howard. *Jesus and the Disinherited.* Boston: Beacon Press, 1996.

West, Cornel. *Race Matters.* New York: Vintage Books, 2001.

Whelchel, L.H. Jr. *The History and Heritage of African American Churches: A Way Out of No Way.* Minnesota: Paragon House, 2011.

Wimberly, Edward P. *African American Pastoral Care.* Nashville: Abingdon Press, 2008.

Windsor, Rudolph R. *From Babylon to Timbuktu: A History of Ancient Black Races Including the Black Hebrews.* Georgia: Windsor's Golden Series, 2003.

ABOUT THE AUTHOR

Dr. Ava S. Harvey, Sr., is the Pastor of the Pilgrim Rest MB Church of Brandon, MS. He is married to Mrs. Leslee B. Harvey and they have two children (Amari and Ava Jr.). Prior to entering full-time ministry, he worked in the Telecommunications industry as a Network Design Administrator and Project Manager.

Pastor Harvey is a sought out speaker that annually frequents multiple revivals, conferences, and workshops. As an effective communicator, he has made presentations to various religious, social, and political groups. He has previously served as a board member of the McKinley Theological Seminary and several community activist organizations. He is a certified mentor through the Mississippi National Guard Youth Challenge Academy and has also volunteered as a "Keys-2-Life" and "Big Brothers & Big Sisters" Mentor for several years.

He is the published author of the "Lighthouse-recognized" book titled *Milk, Manna, and Meat – 90 Days of Spiritual Nourishment* and the Visionary of the FACE-IT Fellowship Ministry.

Pastor Harvey holds a Bachelor of Business Administration from Jackson State University, a Master of Divinity from Wesley Biblical Seminary and a Doctor of Ministry Degree from the Morehouse School of Religion at the Interdenominational Theological Center in Atlanta, Georgia. He is a recipient of the prestigious HEADWAE Academic Excellence Award from the State of Mississippi Legislature. He has also received the distinguished "Pastor of the Year" Honor by the Mississippi Gospel Music Awards. His passion for God and love people is his driving motivation.

Additional Information

For more information concerning the FACE-IT Fellowship contact the ministry:
https://www.facebook.com/faceitfellow/

CPSIA information can be obtained
at www.ICGtesting.com
Printed in the USA
BVHW071618290419
546834BV00005B/621/P